I'm OK

published by HarryMusic © copyright 2025

first published 2025
by P2D Books Ltd

copyright © HarryMusic

A CIP catalogue record of this book is available from the British Library.

ISBN - 978-1-914458-55-2

COVER ARTWORK – THANKS TO ADAM HOWIE

https://www.illusionaryconstructs.com

I'M...OK!

BY

MARC HARRY

For the wonderful ladies in my life - Sarah, Emily and Bronwyn, Eira and Ruth - with love for ever xx

Foreword

Marc Harry shares with us throu of himself and his family that, by virtue reader far richer. Marc has a very frank s and captivating. You won't want to put this book down until you have heard the next instalment as he shares his story of His parents and his siblings and something of the story of The Salvation Army from the perspective of being a child of officers... hence the reference OK 'Officers Kid'.

Marc's memory for detail is fantastic and enlightens the story with such detail that you can imagine yourself in the very place that he is talking about. Not only family members are spoken of but some great heroes of the faith that had influence on a young life that was so profound the names are recorded along with the setting in which they played their part.

The abundant blessing of God is a reccurring theme as is the tenacity and work ethic of officer parents of that age. In the references to his parents the relationship with the ordinary comes across and the relationships that were borne were the bread and butter of the life of a Salvation Army Officer of the time. Ken and Jean Harry cared for their people and ministered to the whole of the community that they were appointed to. That is obvious and found in the pages time after time.

I can personally bear testimony of the generosity of spirit that Ken and Jean showed towards me as a young officer and the warmth and encouragement given. Marc describes the Brinkworth Stamp and thinking back I can see it in action. You will need to read further to know what that means.

If you love a good story - especially if you are interested in some very personal Salvation Army history – you will love this book. The stories contained give credit to the assertion that God does indeed qualify the called in order to serve Him.

So read for yourself, open the pages and enter into the adventure 'Harry' style!

Peter Forrest, Colonel

Chief Secretary

Chapter One - In the Beginning...

All good books start with the line in my chapter heading, don't they? Well...THE 'Good Book' does, at least, and without THAT book I wouldn't be writing this one at all - for the 'OK' in the title refers to 'Officer's Kid': a friendly and informal term for the child of a Salvation Army Officer (or minister) - and I became an 'OK' the moment I entered the world in October 1962. Additionally, though this book tells 'my 'story, the reality is that is is so often the story of my remarkable parents – Ken and Jean Harry – Salvation Army Officers (ministers) for over a century between them!

I need to start this story by going back a generation or two in order to try to put my life as an 'OK' into some sort of historic and cultural perspective. After all, who am I to write this book unless it is in the person of the son of two extraordinary Salvation Army Officers, growing up with them and my sisters in a succession of towns and cities up and down the length of England and Wales? That's where the story lies - that's where we will meet the incredible people I was privileged to share my early, formative years alongside: young and old, sacred and profane, sane and otherwise! And, although we had an extensive Family Tree compiled recently, I promise this opening 'salvo' will not prove an echo of the endless genealogy found in the opening portions of the 'other' book that began with my opening sentence!

This story and, therefore, my own tale begins when William Booth founded The Salvation Army (as The Christian Mission) in 1865 and then eleven years later in Birkenhead when a man called Walter Charles Brinkworth was born. Sometime between then and the end of the 19th century the Brinkworth family moved from one docklands area to another, Cardiff, and in 1897 the 21-year-old Walter married my great-grandmother Alice Maud Duckworth. When they joined Booth's new mission based Christian organisation (for it was never referred to as a church back then!) we do not know, although it would be nice to know if they were both Salvationists or if one joined up when they married – maybe I will find out one day? I do know that they were well established Salvationists by the early 20th Century and that 'Granda Brink', as my dad used to call him, was privileged to carry the Cardiff Grangetown Corps flag at the funeral of William Booth 'The Founder', an event of massive national importance at the time as hundreds of thousands of mourners lined the streets of London to bid farewell to the General.

By the time of that event in 1912, Walter and Alice had brought the first eight of their eventual fifteen children into the world and most of them joined their parents in the Cardiff Grangetown Salvation Army Corps. Only seven of these children survived infancy and their firstborn, Alice died aged just two in 1901.

The seventh of these children was Gwendoline Maud, born on October 9th, 1909. She was my paternal grandmother, the lovely Nana Harry, and I had the honour of being born on her own 53rd birthday - October 9th, 1962. (It is, of course, of great importance that a certain John Lennon beat me to this anniversarian honour - having been born on Nana's 31st...I was merely

reciprocating by being born on his 22nd). To complete the loop, my youngest daughter Bronwyn Gwen (middle name after her Great-Nana) was born on – yes you guessed it – October 9th, 2018.

I wish I knew more about 'Granda Brink' - my dad remembered him well (dad was ten years old when his 'Granda' died in 1940) but he left me with only two other pieces of history:

- He walked with a very particular gait - a heavy-footed one that was known as 'The Brinkworth Stamp' - and many older members of our family frequently reminded dad that he walked in exactly the same way. Dad said that I had it too, as did most of his siblings
- Granda Brink loved to sing 'The Founder's Song'

"O boundless salvation! Deep Ocean of love,
O fullness of mercy, Christ brought from above."

However, whereas most Salvationists would (and still do) clap their hands during the last line of each of the seven verses (and the interspersed refrains of "The Heavenly Gales are Blowing") Granda would make a fist with his right hand and pound the arms of his chair in time with the music. Countless times during my life I watched my father do the same and now, of course, I do it myself! Through some investigations and by comparing to other family photographs we believe Granda Brink is seated 2nd left, arms folded on the Cardiff Grangetown corps photograph shown, with his wife Alice behind him and several, fairly easily identifiable, if one relies on family resemblances, sons and daughters elsewhere in the photograph.

Gwen Brinkworth, who I believe is 2nd from the left (seated) on the front row of the same 1920 photograph (then aged 10 or 11), was married ten years later to Arthur George Harry, a young Christian man from the Hannah Street Mission, just over the River Taff via the nearby Clarence Road bridge.

(Arthur Harry (snr), Eva and my grandfather Arthur (jr) from a family photograph taken in 1914)

Arthur's father (also Arthur George) and his wife Eva had been key workers in the Welsh Revival earlier in the 20th Century whilst worshipping at Loudon Square Church and, when Arthur Sr. died in 1952, he earned the following obituary in the Cardiff Docks Free Churchman magazine:

THE CARDIFF DOCKS FREE CHURCHMAN   October 1952

Mr. Arthur G. Harry

A TRIBUTE

It is with a sense of profound loss that we report the home-call of our dear friend and deacon, Mr. A. G. Harry. He passed peacefully away on Tuesday, September 9th; at the home of his son (232 Corporation Road), and was buried on September 13th. He was aged 76 years.

It was at his own request that the Service was held at Hannah Street Church—to use his own words" . . . where I have spent so many happy hours . . . " and at his request too that there should be flowers from the family only. That other friends should direct their gifts to the Church, in lieu of flowers.

Mr. Harry had been devoted to the Lords' Work, he was indeed "steadfast, unmoved," in the Faith. Never discouraged or upset, never weary in the work. This was no short-lived Christian experience, he had come to know his Lord in his youthful days and his one desire was that the young life of our neighbourhood should come to The Lord. Those who met in the Prayer Meeting will remember his earnest Prayers. He was blessed with a gracious Christian wife and together they worked unceasingly for the Church at Loudoun Square when that Church was a great centre of evangelism. His wife was called Home to her reward early in life, shortly after their attachment to this Church.

For about 24 years Mr. Harry has been a faithful member and prayer warrior of Hannah Street. He has always been a source of spiritual strength and a real "Spiritual Father" in the Faith. This Faith permeated his whole life, to his fellow-drivers, or Dock workers, neighbours and friends he was known as a Christian, but our Brother has now passed to his reward and our Church is the poorer, but heaven is richer. Our district still needs men and women like him . . . his words shortly before passing from this life was that he had " . . . someone to hold on to . . ."

He has indeed laid down his sword and taken up his crown. We join in expressing to his family our sincere prayers and sympathy knowing that they mourn, not without hope, but knowing that Mr. and Mrs. Harry and their daughter Eva too have gone before.

The funeral was conducted and the address given by Mr. A. J. Porter, Mr. Barter and the Salvation Army Officer of Stuart Hall also took part.

Mount Stuart News.

Upon their marriage Arthur jr. joined Gwen in the Salvation Army and my dad, Kenneth Arthur Harry, was born on September 21st, 1930 – he being the eldest of their own eleven children, eight of whom survived infancy. As a family they continued to attend Cardiff Grangetown Corps - and dad often spoke about how many of the black children of the first dockland immigrants from Tiger Bay also used to come and attend the Sunday School.

Amongst them was a little girl, Shirley, who as not much more than a toddler sang on the platform the well-known bible chorus

> *"Now, listen to my tale of Jonah and the whale:*
> *Way down in the middle of the ocean!"*

Dad later watched that little girl's blossoming career closely for the rest of his life, remembering proudly how he had witnessed the first ever public performance of the little girl we now know better as Dame Shirley Bassey!

Little Kenny Harry was 'Army Barmy' from his youngest days and is seen (left) with brothers Trevor and Owen and sister Dorothy. Even then dad was already wearing his 'scarlet jersey' and cap. Gwen, Gwyneth, Peter and Marilyn arrived in turn, by which time the family had moved corps to Cardiff Stuart Hall, right in the City Centre close to the old David Morgan department store.

Dad could only ever recall a limited YP experience - but of course, from the time he was 9, right through to his mid-teens, World War II raged around him - taking its toll on his family as it did every other. Nana Harry's brothers David (Dai) Brinkworth perished on HMS Galatea and William (Billy) on HMS Eclipse while dad's father Arthur held a senior position within the Cardiff Fire Service throughout the war.

Then, one Sunday evening, before the meeting at Stuart Hall, dad was called into the Officer's Room and told,

"Here you are, sign this...you're being 'done' tonight!

That was the extent of my father's 'recruit's classes' or Salvation Army soldiership training! He joined the band, became Deputy Songster Leader in time and had many happy memories of his early years of service in the corps there. The band and songster brigades both undertook regular 'away campaigns' and several photos exist of he and other siblings taking part in these visits. I absolutely love the Stuart Hall Festival Tunics of the day and I would do almost anything in order to acquire one today. I know of only one that still exists so, at least, I may one day get to see it. On the epaulette is a Welsh Dragon and they must have looked splendid with the white, 'lion tamer' stripes across the crimson material!

Dad also remembered his introduction to 'pub booming'. This venture was carried out on Friday and Saturday evenings and involved Salvationists going into the public houses to evangelise and sell copies of the army's newspaper 'The War Cry'. It still happens in some places today but, back then, every corps had a thriving pub-booming ministry. With Grangetown being in the docks area of Cardiff I'm sure you can imagine just how daunting a task this must have been for a young, teenage boy. He particularly remembered one pub 'The House of Blazes' as being particularly rough. History of the area tells us plenty about that establishment and others like 'The Bucket of Blood' and 'The Snakepit' that were well known haunts for brawling sailors and prostitutes!

Away from the Army dad did his apprenticeship as a pattern-maker with Renold Chains. For the final assessment in this training dad made the pattern for the underground conduit that held all the electrical lighting cables for the iconic Skylon Tower – a symbol of the Festival of Britain, 1951 – and an early claim to 'fame' for dad. After completing his apprenticeship and doing his compulsory National Service in REME dad offered to become a Salvation Army Officer.

Cadet Ken Harry entered the International Training College, Denmark Hill (now William Booth College) in 1955 – he became part of "The Swordbearers" session and was commissioned a Lieutenant the next year, being duly packed off to become the Commanding Officer of Eckington Corps in Derbyshire and thence to Youth Officer appointments at Chesterfield, Newcastle City Temple and Liverpool Walton before moving 'overseas' to Ramsey (with Laxey) on the Isle Of Man.

Above - Dad, aged 15, is 2nd from left in this photo of Stuart Hall Songsters taken on a weekend visit to Ware Corps.   Below – the piece of cheese, as Stuart Hall's building was fondly referred to.

Chapter Two - When Nana Got Married she Lost her Voice

If, on my father's side, I am a 4th generation Salvationist then on mum's side I share the same heritage! That would make my children 5th generation and any grandchildren may one day (God-willing) become 6th generation members of the organisation of which their great-great-great 'Granda Brink' carried the flag in its Founder's funeral procession. However, back to my mother's side now…

Henry (known as Edward) Voice was born in 1874. In 1898 Edward Voice married Mary Slee and they were blessed with two sons and then a daughter, Beatrice Bessie (known as Bessie – my Nana Hedges) in January 1916. Sadly, the children's mother Mary died just three years later and Edward remarried giving Bessie a further five siblings (of whom only four survived infancy). Edward and his family moved from Woking to Addlestone and he became the Corps Sergeant-Major at Addlestone Corps.

 In this photograph (from Bessie's younger brother Ron's wedding) Nana is standing beside her father in the centre. Horace, an elder brother is far left and my mother, Jean, is standing at the front between the two boys. Mum's older sister Doreen is a bridesmaid on the right.

Grandad Voice was, by all accounts a great lover of music as well as a multi-instrumentalist and it was, perhaps, only natural that Bessie grew up learning to sing and play the mandolin and concertina. She sang with the songsters, helped with the Sunbeams (a Salvation Army version of Brownies), taught in the Sunday School and became Singing Company (Junior Choir) Leader and later also served as Home League Secretary.

Beatrice

In 1936 she married a local man Charles John Hedges. It was at this point in her long life, of course, that she 'lost her Voice', becoming Bessie Hedges, stalwart of Addlestone Corps, then Hastings Citadel and latterly Addlestone again for a great many years - in fact she was still singing with the songsters until a few weeks before her Promotion to Glory in 2012 at the grand old age of 96. (I used the old family joke about Nana 'losing her voice' to write a comic song for a party we held to celebrate her 80th birthday.)

For many years at Hastings 'Nana Hedges' was a local officer in the corps and particularly served at 'The Lindens Eventide Home, where she faithfully ran a weekly Home League group for several decades.

17

My visits to Hastings as a child were always a treat. Not only did Nana run a very large Guest House (complete with dozens of hiding places, attics and a large dumb waiter) but trips to the Army were a thrill, seeing the band marching with their smart white straps, Grandad Hedges (the Corps Sergeant-Major) was often at the front with the officers and Colour Sergeant – and thus they marched back to the hall for meetings in what was then a large corps with a congregation that, for some time, even included the retired General - Wilfred Kitching.

Mum, outside the family home in Addlestone in which she was born

Charles and Bessie had three daughters, Doreen, Jean and Pauline - the latter pair going on to become Salvation Army officers - and they were active officers through to retirement. Jean, of course, was my mum, Major Jean Harry. With a heritage like mine how could I fail to have been born with anything but Red, Yellow and Blue blood flowing through my veins?

Earlier in her life, once she left school, mum worked in several children's homes as well as in other jobs, including painting seaside ornaments. Most precious to her, though, are the memories from her time at the prestigious 'Claremont' boarding school where wealthy notaries from around the world sent their children to be educated.

Mum entered the ITC in 1959 as a member of the 'Greathearts' session and was commissioned in 1960 to The Salvation Army children's home 'Marshfield' in Southport. The photograph below shows her there with some of the children in Southport, including Fred Schule (to mum's right) who remained a lifelong friend and a kind of 'adopted brother' to my sisters and I. To mum's left is my dad's youngest sister Marilyn – this picture having been taken on the day they first met met, I'm told.

It was while singing with the Southport Corps songster brigade at a divisional event in Liverpool that she was 'spotted' by a single, male officer who, at that time was serving on the Isle of Man...

The story goes that Lieutenant Ken Harry was sat in the gallery of St George's Hall in Liverpool at a Salvation Army Divisional event. As the Southport Songsters sang his eye was drawn to a pretty, young Lieutenant and, very nervously, he asked, afterwards, who she was. Dad must have been very like me (afraid of talking directly to girls) so he eventually found himself addressing the Matron of the children's home and asking her to ask Lt. Jean for permission to write to her! Mum remembers being asked by the Matron if she would like this and, with mum replying in the affirmative, both Matron and the children teased mum daily when the post came to see 'if he'd written yet'. Needless to say 'he' did and they embarked on a fairly short courtship separated, at first, by a stretch of the Irish Sea between Southport and Ramsey

Ken and Jean Harry were married in December, 1961. Dad had been moved back to the 'mainland' the previous May to facilitate his courtship (how kind of the Army) and the wedding took place at Hastings Citadel. So, for a few months

20

at least, they took up their first married appointment in St. Helens...and they began their life together as a couple.

Her first visit to the shops was, I'm told, a rather memorable one for mum! In those pre-equality days she had simply assumed that 'doing the shopping' was the proper, wifely thing to do...but when she returned home with the shopping bags an unexpected inquisition began: "Where did you buy that?" "What did you get that there for...if you'd gone to the other shop you'd have saved a ha-penny!" Consequently, dad did the next shop himself - and then virtually every subsequent shop for the next 41 years. When mum HAD to start shopping after dad's Promotion to Glory in April 2002 all the supermarket check-out operatives wanted to tell her was how sorry they were and how they missed 'their' Mr. Harry. Dad SO loved shopping!

'Yours truly' made my bow in October 1962, as I said earlier it was on Nana Harry's 53rd birthday...and John Lennon's 22nd! But by then St. Helens Par Corps was already in the past - the family had moved to North Wales.

A very precious family photo from early 2011 with five generations of our family - four in SA uniform: Nana Hedges, mum (Jean), me (Marc), Morgan (my eldest son), wife Fiona and their first son Owen.

Chapter Three - Making my Marc

Captains Ken and Jean Harry were appointed to St. Helens Par Corps as their first married appointment but they moved very soon afterwards to Coedpoeth, a little village in North Wales near to Wrexham. It was in the Maelor Hospital, Wrexham that I made my entrance to this world – and have ever since been a proud and patriotic Welshman!

You surely can't expect me to remember much about the 7 months I spent in Denbighshire before the SA, in their wisdom, moved us to Clapham in London, do you? Well, I fully expect that, had I any memory of that winter of 1962/63 I'd have deliberately forgotten it - for I am told it was the coldest and snowiest winter on record in the UK. What a time to be born?

It became family folk-lore that they didn't see the road outside the house from Boxing Day 1962 until Easter 1963. For much of that time conditions were so poor that life ground to a standstill. I can only lay claim to the understanding that exposure to such prolonged cold in the first few months of my life conditioned me for what would come later - for I have ALWAYS preferred being cold to being too hot (unless laying in the sun on a beach, that is).

It is well known that Salvation Army officer salaries in those days were very meagre and this was many decades before the days of central bank accounts and direct salary payments into personal accounts on 'pay-day'. Individual corps paid their officers at that time from their own resources...and, therefore, if the people couldn't get to the corps then they couldn't put any money in the collection plate or make their regular 'cartridge' donations to the Army's work. If there was no money coming into the corps - then none could go out either and, I'm told, many weeks passed without my parents being able to receive their wages that winter.

The corps-folk were most supportive, however, and great friendships were forged in that hard winter – friendships that lasted a lifetime. I remember going back to Coedpoeth on several occasions over the years as I grew up and I was privileged to get to know an ever-dwindling number of friends from the corps on those occasions.

The SA Hall in Coedpoeth was built on a hill with a raised entrance and steps to it on both sides. Of course, it could never be a public building at all in these days of mandatory access for disabled etc. and it was sad to see the old hall empty, rather derelict and up for sale last time I visited with mum to do the weekend's meetings about twelve years ago. The corps is, however, still there - now sharing a lovely worship hall with another church.

The living quarters now ascribed to army officers, too, is rather better than the (literally) rat-infested holes they were, at times, then! Mum and dad used to have to put mesh sheets up over my pram to stop the rats getting to me. Mind you, I'm told that Nana Harry didn't exactly help with the decor! She came up from Cardiff to help mum after she'd brought me home from hospital. Never

having had a gas cooker of her own Nana showed a fine example of the 'try something first and if it doesn't work ask for help' mentality so beloved of us Harrys! She put a saucepan on the hob and turned on the gas - but when she returned a few minutes later and noticed it still wasn't lit she struck a match...and blew out the kitchen window! Oops!!

Talking about the dire monetary situation necessitates mention of one further example of the absolute perfection of God's timing. It's not only food you can't buy without money - you also cannot pay your utility bills. The Electricity Board had been chasing a bill of just over £5 for much of the winter...most worrying in freezing weather for the young, helpless parents of a five month old baby. One day, the morning post arrived and the very first letter was a Final Demand - "unless this bill is paid today we will be cutting off your electricity supply". Despair. Another envelope from the same delivery was, this time, from Salvation Army National Headquarters - and contained a completely unexpected Five Pound note for every officer - to help them with heating bills in the vicious winter. No matter how many times we are let down by other people we are reminded that God will NEVER let us down.

He knows just what we need before we even ask Him, says the Bible - and here was the perfect example, courtesy of Headquarters and the Post Office.

Coedpoeth Songsters – in their familiar Salvation Army uniforms and also, below, in traditional Welsh costume

I cannot leave Coedpoeth without telling you about Aunty Iett (short for Harriett). Herbert and Harriett Williams had not long been married when a serious mining accident made it impossible for him to father children and this had, of course, been a great sadness to them for many years. They had no connection with The Salvation Army at all, with the exception of living near to the officer's quarters and, therefore being neighbours of my parents.

By all accounts Aunty 'Iett doted on me from the day I came home with mum from the hospital. She would take me out for walks, wrapping me up warm in the traditional Welsh nursing shawl which is worn by mothers to carry their babies. One day, after such a walk, Aunty 'Iett handed me back to my mother with a confession,

"I was in the shop with Marc and a lady came in very surprised. 'Ooh Iett.' she said, 'I didn't know you were expecting a baby!' 'Neither did I,' I replied,. 'I thought I only had the flu!'"

Aunty 'Iett and Uncle Herbert were every bit my second parents and we always made sure we visited them every time we returned to the village in years to come. I was fooled for years by Uncle Herbert once convincing me that he could 'read' what music was on a 78 record by closely examining the grooves - yes, it was years before I realised I'd been had!

Sadly, Herbert died in the late 1970s and dad was invited back to conduct his funeral. After the service we took Aunty 'Iett home with us for a week or so in Tunstall where she came with us to the Army and she must have realised what she'd been missing all these years. For, once back in Coedpoeth, she began attending the corps and she spent the rest of her life as a uniformed Salvationist. God knows His time - and His work in 'Iett's life took a long time to reach fruition, but "Praise Him!" it did just that!

In that long, cold and penniless winter mum and dad often wondered who it was that had left baskets of groceries on their doorstep when there was no money to buy any. Thank God for 'Iett and Herbert Williams, for it was they who had done so all the time - two great early influences on my life, whose kindness, generosity of spirit and willingness, albeit somewhat unknowingly, to do the will of God marked my life forever.

I only recently found this lovely photograph 'Iett and Herbert with her 'dose of flu'.

Chapter Four - Uncle Mac and a "Cockney Sparrer"

At the beginning of writing this chapter I found myself wondering how on earth I was going to fill more than a few lines on the period of my life that covered May 1963 (when I was a mere seven months old) to the same month in 1965 - for my initial memories of Clapham consisted of little more than picking up an old blind lady called Miss Tozer for the Over-60s club and a sudden, vivid picture of a cot and some patterned wallpaper that flashed subconsciously into my mind in Autumn 1991 the first time I opened a box of Farley's Rusks. They were for my first-born son, Morgan to eat, just a few months after I became a dad myself and the smell of the biscuits I used to eat as a baby, so many years ago, had woken that long-imprisoned memory! What an incredible thing the human mind is!

Oh...and I could also mention the most bizarre recurring dream that anyone I ever met has heard! That dream began in Clapham...

I'd love to be able to tell you how living in the hustle and bustle of London made such an incredible contrast with life in a hilly North Welsh village...but, really, I can't! I find it rather frustrating that a head so absolutely crammed full of just about everything that ever happened to me from Bargoed up to the present day should have a four-year 'virtual void' from 1963 to 1967. On the other hand I was barely 4½ years old by the end of that 'void' - so I know I have an excuse!

I can remember Mrs. Hughes. She always seemed to be a hundred years old so, returning to Clapham to see her several years later, when she'd finally reached that goal, was a little bizarre in itself. That must have been late in 1970 for dad also took me into Clapham High Street to visit a record shop where a lady who used to sell him records offered me 'the pick of the shop'! What would I choose? (If I gave you a hundred guesses you wouldn't get there...and, as a by-product, all my hard-earned 'music cred' would be straight out of the window!)

Old Mrs. Hughes was Number One on the Clapham Corps roll - dad always had a special affinity with the elderly folk in each corps he officered - and Mrs. Hughes was no exception. In another cold and snowy spell he felt compelled to find out if Mrs. Hughes was alright. This was long before our family ever had a car so, as always, he ventured out onto the icy roads on his old, black pushbike. I remember dad frequently using the old advertising phrase, "Where there' s a need - there's The Salvation Army!" and he lived out that expression every day of his life. Mrs. Hughes and her other neighbours were, effectively, housebound by the snow so dad spent all day clearing the snow from not only her path but all the neighbours paths as well - then he went out and did all their shopping too! To me that was every bit as much part of his Salvation Army officership as was the preaching and management of corps life - it was also walking up and down the High Street in full uniform a few times a day just in case anyone needed him...and SO often they did!

I vaguely remember my little playmate Olu! I'm going to attempt a guess at spelling what mum told me was her full name: Olufamuyeyo Kayeyo! The family joke has always been that Olu was my 'first girlfriend'. Ha ha! Maybe I should explain how we came to know her... it's quite a bizarre tale – for, surely the SA Quarters situation my parents found themselves in at Clapham was unique even in the 'good old Army'.

The previous officers at the corps had asked permission for the wife's parents to move in with them and had been given that permission as long as, of course, when the time came for them to move on to any new appointment the in-laws moved too. For some reason, though, this didn't happen, so mum and dad and I moved into a house with 'sitting tenants'. We lived upstairs in two bedrooms with a kitchen/diner and the Stevensons lived downstairs in two more bedrooms, a kitchen, a lounge and a bathroom.

This couple fostered Olu. The baby's mother had come to the UK from Africa, seemed to settle well and attended the corps but then suddenly made the decision to return home - she left her daughter in England in the hope of her having a better life and so Olu lived with our 'neighbours'. I must confess I have no idea where my 'girlfriend' is today but my parents picked up regular reports for some time and the last they heard she had done well in school and was working at Harrods. I hope that justified her mother's decision at least to some extent.

Because we didn't have 'custody' of the house bathroom we used to make regular trips to 'Alver Bank', where we were able to bathe! I remember Alver Bank - it was a Salvation Army Old People's home that obviously came under Clapham Corps 'district' and, therefore, mum and dad would have visited regularly anyway to see the old folk who lived there. I vaguely remember once being there with Santa (so I guess that was Christmas?) and I have a picture in my mind of one particular lady, rather rotund and in a pale blue blouse who had the most enormous goitre on her neck - the fact I remember it now so clearly obviously means that I must have been, at the time, an utterly embarrassing tot who had stared at the poor old dear for ages. Sorry mum and dad!

But the main things I both associate with Clapham and remember about it are my sister Eira and Uncle Mac! If my parents hadn't had enough of snow in the winter that I was born they didn't show it when they then decided to name my first sister after it! For Eira is Welsh for snow! As soon as I discovered this fact I began to wonder why, if her first name is Eira then why is her middle name Jane? Why not Siân? And if Jane then why not 'Snow'?

This dichotomy obviously troubled me greatly throughout my life for I then began to be grateful the Registrar had assumed my name was Marc (not Mark) as there is no letter 'k' in the Welsh alphabet. But then - why was my dad Kenneth and not Cennydd when registered in Cardiff? Why was my middle name Owen and not Owain? Have I been OCD ever since childhood? (Answer: almost certainly "yes" but who knew about the Autism Spectrum in the early 1960s?)

Mum gave birth to Eira in the army's own 'Mother's Hospital' in Hackney (within the sound of Bow Bells) making my little sister a true cockney. Eira has always been intensely proud of her London roots and, when she left home, many years later there was only ever one place she was going to go to live! The 'Mother's' meant nothing to me, in particular, for many years - until I became interested in football, in fact - and then I learned that a whole plethora of football stars shared Eira's birthplace. The first one I remember discovering this about was Ron 'Chopper' Harris, erstwhile Chelsea captain, back in the day when the club still had a few English players AND those players were allowed to 'tackle' properly! Chopper Harris would have broken a modern player's leg by simply LOOKING at him! If they had ever started a game together on opposing teams I can think of a few modern players who might have run half way back to their homeland by the time the referee had put his whistle back in his pocket from the kick-off!

But mum wasn't the only one who spent time in hospital during our stay in London. One evening, while watching a TV programme called 'Your Life In Their Hands' my dad had become intrigued by a new operation shown on the programme. The Harrys have always had fragile hearing (I think I'm right in saying that at least seven of dad's eight siblings wear or wore a hearing aid). Years of apprenticeship in a noisy workshop filled with lathes and grinders followed by National Service with tanks and guns (not to mention playing trombone in Army bands) had already taken their toll on dad's ears so he asked his doctor if the TV operation might be of use to him. He was recommended for the operation and the tiny bones of his inner ear (hammer, anvil and stirrup) were replaced by a stainless steel piston, restoring a large amount of his hearing for the next few years.

I believe the first time he went out after the operation was to push Eira's pram in the park - he kept asking mum what it was he could hear? Mum had to explain that it was birds in trees, an aeroplane buzzing overhead...that sort of thing - sounds he could never remember hearing before! The operation proved to have a 'time limitation', however, and, although dad was very deaf by the time he died, that was another 40 years hence. Fortunately, his hearing deficiencies never lessened his love of music even if he did frequently miss whole chunks of conversations!

And so to 'Uncle Mac'. Most SA corps have someone who dad would have described as the 'Head Cook and Bottle-Washer'. Mac was this man at Clapham. Officially the CSM he was also acting Bandmaster and much more besides. His wife Jenny had been Home League Secretary. Most of what I, personally, associate with Uncle Mac comes from long after the days when mum and dad were corps officers at Clapham SA, though. Adam McCaig was, without doubt, one of the most impressive, powerful and imposing men it has ever been my privilege to meet and always one of our greatest family friends. Imagine a Scottish Rugby Union prop forward with all the height, muscle and power you'd associate with that and couple it with a striking presence, dominant self-belief and a voice like Dad's Army's Private Fraser in the middle of a 'We're Doomed' monologue...and you might be half way there!

Mac and his lovely wife Jenny had spent the majority of their lives being missionaries for The Salvation Army in various parts of India - most notably the Punjab. Mac's slide shows brought to life a part of the world I have never visited and it was he that shared with my young mind both the majesty and the contrasting squalor of life in India. These gave me a glimpse of Christian/Hindu and Muslim relationships long before the modern, political world made us much more aware! Mac was a mesmerising man and I so wish I could spend just a few hours in his presence again today!

He had the sort of voice that, when he spoke, could transfix you for hours at a time and, when he sang, transport you to Heavenly realms. "Down From His Glory" to the tune of 'O Sole Mio' was his song - and if Pavarotti ever sang it more compellingly then I have yet to hear the recording! Uncle Mac was one of those men who made it worth moving house and corps every two years - for each move meant he would be back to visit the next stopping place* as the special guest for a Young People's anniversary weekend or Self-Denial (Annual Apeal) Sunday!

*Mum and dad had a plaque to put up on each house they lived in - a Greek word 'Proskairon' - meaning 'for a little while'. Each 'little while' meant Uncle Mac would be coming back soon!

As I wrote earlier they became great family friends - two of the very best - and Mac and Jenny's home in Thurleston Avenue, Morden (the address is ingrained in my memory) was always an open door to members of our family. Jenny cooked the most incredible authentic Indian cuisine - and she could prepare a meal with a common or garden cucumber that lesser chefs could have never dreamed of!

By the time I played the organ for Mac's funeral (dad led the service) poor Jenny's mind had already begun to be ravaged by the terrible effects of Alzheimer's but we shed tears together as I belted out 'O Sole Mio' on a pretty 'naff' Bontempi organ with enough verve to make it sound like the Albert Hall!

Adam McCaig (Uncle Mac) in his Indian costume

Chapter Five - Mad...or Dad?

There is one story from the Clapham appointment that, without a doubt, deserves its own chapter. It is the sort of story that, if it happened today, would make newspaper headlines and, perhaps, my dear dad would have had received a medal or some other commendation. Yet, this story has never been told in public before - which is typical of Ken Harry's self-effacing humility and the fact he took incidents like this as just a normal part of life. For most of us, thank God, they are not - but for a man of courage and principles, like dad, they were just things to be met face on and dealt with as efficiently as possible.

There was a couple associated with the corps in Clapham that in yet more ways showed the ever-growing cosmopolitan nature of London's populace in the early 1960s:

- He was Ukrainian (Russian in those days) and had fled his homeland years before in search of a better life. He had tried living in the USA but, having not found it suited to him, he had moved to London to try there instead. He had left behind a wife and family in the Ukraine many years ago and had never had any contact with them since he left.

- She had been brought up in pre-war Germany, had been forced to be part of the Hitler-Youth project with all the horror and mental scarring that that entailed - being forced to run naked through the woods at gunpoint etc. As a result of the trauma and guilt associated with this she had suffered several breakdowns over the years.

Although she was a lot younger than the Ukrainian man they had met and eventually established a long-term relationship. In order that they might marry he wrote to the authorities to seek permission - he having been married previously in his homeland. The authorities tried to find out if his former wife was still alive and, having found no record of her in the Ukraine, the couple were given official, legal consent to wed.

All was well for quite some considerable time but, one day, completely out of the blue, a letter arrived at their home - and it was from his first wife! What a horror that must have been in so many ways for them. He felt obliged to make contact with her and, consequently, made arrangements to travel back to the Ukraine. He reassured his new wife that she had nothing to worry about and that he would be back within a fortnight. Unfortunately, her fragile psyche found this hard to accept and, to confuse matters even further, her ex-partner from more than ten years before found her at the same time her husband left for Ukraine. This led to her having another breakdown and she was left very vulnerable.

Within the two weeks her husband was absent she had the authorities annul her marriage and, further, went ahead and married her ex-partner! As he had promised the old man returned from Russia - to find the locks changed on his house and his 'wife' now married to someone else! By the time the situation came to came to my parents (and the police's) attention he had forced his way into the house with a gun and was effectively holding the newlyweds hostage.

Dad went to the house and found the police outside, holding a watching vigil with a megaphone and awaiting further forces for assistance to deal with the situation. As was his wont, though, dad let the police officer in charge of the situation know of his frustration as to why it hadn't yet been resolved.

"I'm going in," he said - and was told in no uncertain terms that he most certainly was NOT 'going in' anywhere!

"Don't be daft," said dad. "I know them all!" And 'in' he marched.

Once inside the house he spoke to the occupants, diffused the situation and calmly but authoritatively took the gun from the hostage-taker. They all walked out a few minutes later to an utterly bemused police force. I'm told this most unusual 'ménage a trois' subsequently all lived together: the old man in the daughter's bedroom, the new couple in his old marital bedroom and the daughter on the couch! Truly, it takes all sorts to make a world!

THAT was my dad - no fuss, wanting no praise - just getting the job done. I believe he did something quite similar many years later on an aeroplane in Yugoslavia at the time of its developing civil war when he felt responsible for a holiday party he had taken on a corps holiday and upon their being detained by the militia...but that's another story for another book!

Mad or dad? Most definitely a bit of both, bless him...and I've always been extremely proud to be his son!

Well...Clapham didn't do so badly in filling a chapter after all did it, then?

What?

That record? (Do I have to...?)

OK - given the pick of the whole shop I asked for Lee Marvin grunting 'Wanderin' Star' in his bourbon and tobacco-soaked 'basso profundo' from the musical 'Paint Your Wagon'! Maybe it was not such a bad choice - the B-side is one of only two recordings I know of with Clint Eastwood singing! I had an eye for a rarity even then...and that's my excuse, like it or lump it!

What's that? You want to know about the recurring dream as well? Ho-hum...well, it really was quite scary at the time...I was in the London Underground looking across at one of those very long, old, wooden escalators. This one was descending and everyone I knew was on it, standing single file with their mouths open, teeth removed and a whole, unshelled walnut in their cakehole - even poor old blind Miss Tozer was there.

I know I had the dream many times and it left me with a life-long legacy of hating seeing friends and family without their false teeth in! Sometimes, even today, if someone loses a tooth or crown I can hardly look at them! Interpret that, if you will!

The Salvation Army Mothers' Hospital where my sister and many famous Londoner's were born. It was a very similar establishment to the one depicted in nearby Poplar in the BBC series 'Call the Midwife'.

Chapter Six - And Your New Appointment...Has No Hall!

May 1965 arrived, 'moving time' for Salvation Army Officers and their families, and the Harrys were heading back over the Severn Bridge to Casnewydd! Or so I always thought until I discovered much later that the said bridge wasn't even opened until 1966! That's the problem with these early chapters - my own memories up to this point are a bit vague to say the least but, fortunately, my dad loved to tell me stories about things he'd done as I was growing up and my dear mum also had a very good and retentive memory until the last few years of her life when, sadly, it was diminished by the ravages of dementia!

By the next move, two years later, I can remember lots myself but, I have to confess, I needed some of those recollections of my parents - after all, even by the time of the move from Clapham to Newport Central I was still only just over two and a half years old!

I can remember the SA house (we call them 'Quarters') was in a very long road in the west of Newport and also the fact that it was not too far from the famous Transporter Bridge over the River Usk. I recall the back garden and the fact it had a low wall between a concrete area and a raised lawn (more of the wall later!) and I remember the first of what must have been many, many hundreds of football matches I attended with my dad - on that occasion to Somerton Park, the old ground of Newport County, where they wore yellow and black scarves and sang, "Roll up and see the County play!"

I can clearly remember walking (by myself!) to the barbershop just around the corner from our house and I remember the barber himself: old, bald and wearing a white coat like a scientist. I had to ask for 'short back and sides' and, after sitting like a good boy throughout the procedure, I was always rewarded with a Fox's Glacier Mint. I can just as clearly recall going to watch athletics at Maindee Stadium and seeing the great Lynn Davies jump so far that he almost came out of the end of the long-jump pit! They extended it soon afterwards, I'm told!

I can remember starting Nursery and the fact there were little beds there so we younger ones could have a 'nap' when tired and also the shock I got one day when a friend turned up at Nursery completely bald - I'm guessing it was because of the dreaded hair-lice but nobody explained it back then!

I have been told that my insatiable love for music really began to take a hold at this time. Having climbed up a cupboard to where I could reach my father's turntable I had tried to put on an LP of Walt Disney music – with the result that I scratched the said record badly. As a result I was bought a wind-up gramophone and a very random selection of 78 RPM records to play on it. I remember some were duplicates of Salvation Army 78s that my dad had, others included Mickey Mouse club songs, monologues by Music Hall comedian Sandy Powell and a very silly song called 'Cocktails for Two' by an American novelty act called Spike Jones and his City Slickers.

My favourite piece of music at that time, though, was 'The Harry Lime Theme' from the film The Third Man. I had the record amongst my 78s and played it (so I'm told) endlessly on my gramophone. Well, I did until one sunny afternoon when I took it off my turntable and placed it on that little brick wall in the garden for a moment. My sister, Eira, promptly sat on it and it snapped in half!

Apparently, I was inconsolable...and part of me probably jokes I still haven't completely forgiven her for this wanton act of vandalism all these years later...

I jest, of course - for the very fact Eira survived our stay in Newport at all is something we have all given thanks for many times in the 55 years and more between now and then.

It was December 1965 and Eira was still under two years old. I had caught measles, been properly diagnosed and was on the way to recovery when she also fell ill. It seemed obvious that she'd caught the same virus - but the doctor, when called upon disagreed. Consequently, Eira became even more ill and the doctor was called again - with the same result.

You see, the measles rash, so familiar now to all of us, just hadn't appeared and the doctor had now said twice that she was not of the opinion that Eira had measles. Finally, on New Year's Eve, as Eira lay listless and nearly lifeless on the settee my parents called the surgery once more asking if, this time, they could send a different doctor and, a short while later, the doctor duly arrived - in his evening suit with his family in the car with him! The family were, we were told, in their best bib and tucker and on their way to a New Year's Eve party. I am eternally grateful to them that they stopped on the way!

When the doctor examined Eira he asked if his father (also a doctor) might come in and help with his diagnosis - so Eira was seen by two doctors at once, the result being that she was taken immediately to hospital with measles and, by that time, pneumonia as well. The problem had arisen due to the measles rash only manifesting itself internally which is far from common, I'm told. I do recall that, many years later, when Eira's adult teeth came through there was some discolouration evident that had been caused all those years earlier by that missing rash!

The doctors were not exaggerating when they admitted that, had they not been called that very evening, Eira would not have lived through the night. Once in hospital she was taken into an isolation unit and there received the treatment she needed to make a recovery. Thank God for His goodness to us on that occasion!

Less than a year later my parents were to be part of an event that led to many other families being far less fortunate than we had been - for mum and dad both played vital roles in the nearby Aberfan disaster in October 1966.

Every year Salvation Army officers from all around the country at that time made their way to a gathering with other officers in Swanwick, Derbyshire, an event known in the Army as 'Officers Councils'. It was while they were driving back from a few days at councils that news broke about the famous incident, in which an old slag-heap (pile of coal dust) on top of a mountain overlooking the valleys village of Aberfan had become waterlogged and slipped down the mountainside on top of the village school soon after the school day had begun. 116 children and 28 adults died that day, buried in the black sludge that engulfed them. People had been warning for several years about the threat of such a slippage, but the time for recriminations was far into the future as this awful tragedy unfolded on that tragic morning.

Dad stopped at home only long enough to change out of his SA uniform and into an old boiler suit before setting off straight away for

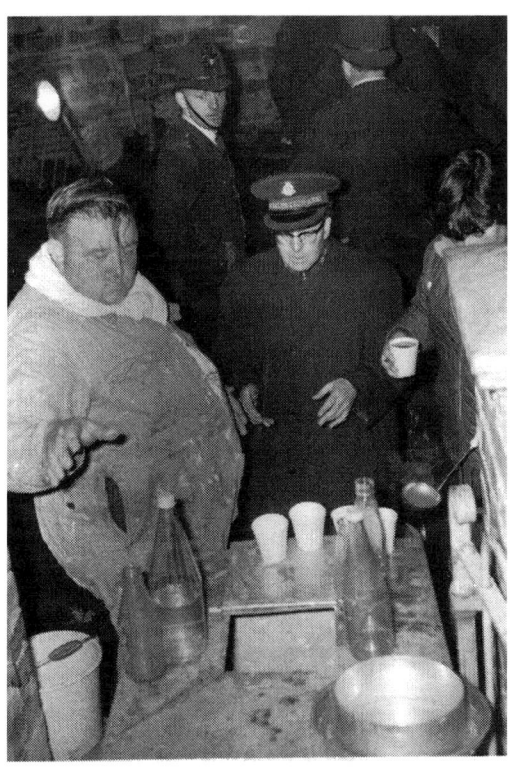

Aberfan, where he was personally to carry the bodies of 26 of those children from the school to the church that was used as a temporary morgue. He laid each of their little bodies on the pews to be identified by grieving parents not by their faces but by the clothes they had worn to school that fateful morning.

Dad (above left, in that boiler suit) was there for 6 days and 5 nights before returning home. Mum only visited the scene once but collected tins of food and other essentials locally in Newport to take with her to Aberfan in order to help the emergency services and the many other volunteers helping to deal with the aftermath of the disaster.

I think you will understand when I say that, of all the things my dad did as a Salvation Army officer in his many years' service I am more proud of the part he played in the Aberfan tragedy than anything else.

I've been aware of that disaster for as long as I can remember and, much as I would love to think I could have done what he did I seriously doubt I could ever have done that. I'm sure there would have been much more to report here had dad not found it virtually impossible to talk about this event throughout the rest of his life – but I could not be any more proud of him and his involvement. I went back to the site of the old Pantglas School a few years ago and sat with my wife and daughter in the Memorial Garden that is now on that site.

(Below: two of dad's own photographs from Aberfan)

I've managed to write about Newport so far without once mentioning the corps my parents were stationed at - Newport Central. It doesn't exist now, having merged with the other Newport corps, Maindee, in 1995. Sadly, I cannot remember a single thing about the corps at all, apart from the name of one bandsman who kindly gave me a leather football and a brother and sister who used to babysit Eira and I when mum and dad went out.

However, I am told that it was a happy corps with a dozen or so in the band and with a songster brigade to match. What they didn't have during mum and dad's stay in Newport...was a hall!

Even with what I subsequently learned about the weird and wonderful world of Salvation Army property I find it hard to believe this series of events actually happened - but I'm assured it did. Mum and dad's predecessor at the corps seemed to have simply made the rather bizarre decision to sell the hall to a property developer! Yes, really! There was no discussion had with National Headquarters or even the more local Divisional Commander – just the sale!

The property developer concerned was trying to buy all the buildings in that part of the town in order to have the space to place a new development and the sum involved was somewhere near £32,000 (a very considerable sum in 1965). The developers had done nothing with the old SA hall, though, with the exception of removing the stairs...and they were very slow it transpired in actually handing over the said £32k!

Of course, until the corps had the money they could not start work on a replacement hall - so where, you might think, were the corps meant to worship? (I still find myself asking how on earth this ever happened?) Dad found an old carpet salesroom and gained permission to use it but it was very dirty and unkempt, so he organised a good old 'Army Scrubology' on the Saturday and they got the room presentable.

Unfortunately, the salesroom also had an upstairs, and that was used on the Saturday evening for a discotheque - which duly caused more of the ceiling below to collapse and, when they arrived for worship on Sunday morning the room was almost as dirty and dusty as it had been before the 'scrubology'.

There was also neither platform nor pulpit - only a bar - so mum and dad laid their sessional flags (the flags worn by officers whilst being commissioned/ordained) over the bar and preached from there and agreed that somewhere else, more suitable, simply had to be found!

The next week the Army started worshipping at the local YMCA, borrowing the hall for Sundays and one afternoon and evening a week, during which the Home League and Over-60s meetings and all sectional rehearsals had to take place - but at least they now had a 'home'.

The problem remained of the unpaid £32,000 and any prospect of a new hall. Fortunately for Newport Central Captain Ken Harry, as we have seen already, was not a man prepared to be messed about! He rang Divisional Headquarters in Cardiff every week for updates on progress and, finding no success there, he began to make regular contact with the

SA Property Offices at 101 Queen Victoria Street, London - the National (now Territorial) Headquarters. Yet, still, he had no success in obtaining answers. It was all very frustrating for him and all concerned with the corps, of course.

Then, one day, while visiting his parents in Cardiff dad met his cousin, George Brinkworth, in a street in the city centre measuring a building with some other policemen. George (whose father Sam Brinkworth was the son of Walter, my great-grandfather and a former soldier at Cardiff Grangetown Corps as mentioned earlier) was a Detective Constable with Cardiff Police who later went on to be a founding member of the Cardiff Drugs Squad. I remember dad often bumping into 'big George' as he walked around the city streets and they would often chat for, what seemed to me as a small child, hours before we could move on!

Back at that time, though, George was working with CID – and, it transpired, he was working on a fraud case involving some rogue property developers who were buying up city properties for less than their true value (by measuring wrongly and, hence, paying for too little square footage) and who were also, seemingly, reluctant to actually pay for the properties thus acquired!

When George happened to mention the firm's name it became clear to dad that this was the same firm who had performed the same trick earlier in Newport! Coincidence or God-incidence? George took some details and promised to make his cousin's problem a priority - and he was good to his word. A few weeks later he sent dad a letter with confirmation of the Newport SA payment having been made in full!

However, word seemed to taking rather longer to filter through to Queen Victoria Street in London. Again and again dad phoned and still they insisted,

"As soon as we hear anything or receive any money we'll let you know."

At this point, dad held a meeting at the corps with the finance local officers and the decision was made to take the letter from George Brinkworth with them and visit "101" themselves. So, a few days later, three uniformed Salvationists caught the train to London and walked into the property offices at NHQ later that morning, where they were told, quite firmly, that they could not see anyone without an appointment.

"Well, we're not going anywhere," they replied - and they didn't. All day! When everyone except the manager had eventually gone home he must have realised that he'd have to talk to them and he finally came out, repeating what by now had become something of a mantra,

"As soon as we hear anything or receive any money we'll let you know."

Dad presented him with the letter from South Wales Police with the date of payment, the account number of the account it had been paid into, the cheque number and the names of the two signatories on the cheque. Maybe word hadn't yet reached that office in Queen Victoria

Street but that poor manager could not believe his eyes that day. Apologies no doubt followed and building work commenced shortly afterwards. As I wrote above, Ken Harry was not a man to be messed about; he might not have always made himself universally popular either - but he did usually get things done!

One final story my mum remembered from Newport concerned the world famous shop, Marks and Spencer. As often happened with Salvation Army corps for many years M&S used to contact The Salvation Army at the close of a day's business in order to donate unsold food to the organisation. Someone needed to be by a telephone at a certain time of day and, if they had anything for the Army it would be collected and used to distribute and use as appropriate. It was the last day of business before Christmas and the phone call came, with an added request,

"Could you possibly get two cars as there might be a lot today?"

So dad rang Captain Gordon Kent, the officer from Newport Maindee, and they both drove to the shop. A little interpolation here that I recall - Captain Kent was tall and thin while Captain Harry was shorter and somewhat rounder. In their dark, navy suits they really did resemble Laurel and Hardy! We had a pair of Laurel and Hardy figures at home that were forever known to us children as dad and Gordon Kent! But I digress...when they arrived at the shop they found staff loading up a lorry with more Christmas goodies than could be imagined: chickens, turkeys, cakes, puddings, vegetables, breads, cream...the parade of pallets seemed endless and dad and Gordon turned to each other and joked,

"There's not going to be much left for us at this rate!"

As they closed the back doors of the lorry the manager turned to dad and said,

"Right that's it! Where do you want it delivered?"

The lorry was all for the Army...at 6pm on Christmas Eve! What could they do?

The lorry was eventually driven to our house in Mendalgief Road where the food filled the whole front room and passageway. Officers from every corps in the division were told to visit and take whatever they could use and all elderly and needy families known to the

corps were visited that night and given hampers of goodies before Christmas.

When the band went out playing carols the next morning, Christmas Day, mum loaded up a big double push-chair with food and tried giving it away to passers-by who put money in the collecting tin - but to little avail – everyone, it seemed, had everything 'in' for Christmas that they needed already! No-one ever said that a Salvation Army officer's life was not a full and varied one!

(There is one more, rather wonderful story that I was told concerning food donated by Marks and Spencer on a different occasion. Dad received the usual phone call from M&S the night before they left for Officers Councils in Swanwick – as mentioned above). Although he managed to deliver most of what was donated to the Army on that occasion there was one box of Cherry Pies that remained in the car.

Anyway, the story involved a very dear friend of our family - Retired Brigadier Reg Hayman – he became, a few years later, the man who enrolled me as a Senior Soldier in 1976.

Now, this was in the days when there was no food at all provided for guests after the evening meal had finished...and the pickings that particular year at evening meal, I'm told, were particularly scrawny. ALL the officers were rather hungry come mid-evening...so much so that, in the end, Reg took to his bedroom to go and pray for manna! Lest he be disturbed he took out his much needed hearing aids.

Of course, my parents had, in the boot of their car, those same Cherry Pies that had been kindly donated by M&S – so they took one to each officer at councils that evening. Knocking on Brigadier Hayman's door dad heard whispered prayer and, not wishing to disturb the saint during his devotions, he left the pie on the bedspread at which he knelt.

(Brigadier Reg Hayman – such a wonderful Man of God – and devotee of Heavenly cherry pies!)

Not long later the officers gathered downstairs heard shouting and a large commotion in the distance. There were cries of "It's a miracle!" and "The Lord has answered my prayers!"

Lo and behold, the Brigadier arrived downstairs some time later, and to everyone else's great amusement, was absolutely elated at this very obviously physical answer to his prayers.

How I wish I'd been there to witness that scene unfold!!!!)

Chapter Seven - Bargoed, Starting School and my First Awareness of God and the 'Army'

With the work ready to begin on building the new hall in Newport it was time for us to be 'on the move' once again. We didn't have a long journey ahead of us this time, though; in fact we travelled a mere 17 miles in a north-westerly direction into the Rhymney Valley and the town of Bargoed, near the castle town of Caerphilly.

Bargoed had sprung up in the early Twentieth Century when a large coal mine was opened there in 1903. The mine, like all others in South Wales has now long gone and the site has been preserved as a beautiful country park. Bargoed can count amongst its famous children the actress Doris Hare (On the Buses), boxer Nathan Cleverly and many members of the singing group Only Boys Aloud.

When the Harrys arrived in May 1967, however, the mines were still very much at the heart of the communities found in the valleys of South Wales. The streets had that omnipresent grimy, black coating that settled there from the smoky, smoggy air and coal dust. Trudging up Church Street twice a day on the way home from school very much conjures up images for me of the old Hovis advert from TV. It is one of the steepest, inhabited roads in the country.

I suppose, from a Salvation Army perspective, appointing my father to Bargoed Corps was something of a brave move – for his own younger brother Trevor was the Songster Leader at the corps and Trevor and Ivy's own young family were all very keenly involved. Thus I got to spend the next two years with my cousins Janet and Graham, Uncle Trevor and Aunty Ivy – the only time that I ever spent living near to relations other than my immediate family!

Bargoed Corps is, perhaps, most famous in Salvation Army circles for the eponymous march, composed in 1932 by BM Courtney Bosanko, featuring the chorus 'I Believe in the Word of God' and still occasionally played today. Bargoed had also had a very good band for most of its history and, from what I recall, still had a keen and competent one in the late 1960s numbering about 15-20 players. The photograph below is from a 1923 postcard – quite a formidable band in those days!

Because I was aged between 4 and 6 during the period we lived there I am much more aware of memories of people, places and events that took place and lots of the corps-folk hold (or held) a dear place in my heart for their words, deeds and the relationships I developed with some of them (even at such a tender age) so very long ago.

Placed firmly at the top of that list of names is Corps Sergeant Major Ted Stephens, a man I didn't know for very long at all as he was 'Promoted to Glory' during the time we lived in the town. But Ted was, to me, an early 'faith hero'... Do you know, I cannot recall him ever even speaking a single word to me (I'm sure he did, I just don't remember) but his 'presence', the aura of holiness that seemed to surround him and the following experiences earned him that esteemed place in my memory.

Ted (seen on the photograph - front left - marching in front of Portsmouth Citadel Band on their weekend visit for the Rhymney Valley Festival in 1968) could have been lifted straight out of an Army meeting in 1910 and dropped into Bargoed hall on a Sunday morning for all I knew! His uniform was old – not just an upright tunic – everyone had those in 1966 – but with navy, lion-tamer stripes across the tunic. Long-service medals, gleaming silver with red ribbons gave him the look of a living history book; and the first I saw of him every Sunday morning was kneeling at his seat on the platform in fervent prayer. I remember asking my mum, one Sunday, why he was doing that when the meeting hadn't even started yet? It seemed a bizarre thing for a man to do to in the eyes of a very small child! Mum answered kindly that it was a thing that some Salvationists liked to do to help prepare them for the day's worship – so Ted was my first direct link to the old Army 'knee drill' and I'll always remember him on one knee, a hand steadying himself on the old, wooden chair and the other clasped to his forehead, amongst his white hair, deep in prayer.

It was a visit to Ted's house one day while accompanying dad on some 'visiting' that left the deepest impression on me, though; my own dad was a great worker – even in the few corps we were ever at that failed to appreciate him fully there was never anyone who wouldn't acknowledge how hard and tirelessly he worked; at Bargoed I can still see him single-handedly putting those old-fashioned, heavy wooden trestle tables up and down on his own, decorating (I wouldn't be surprised if he wallpapered every room of every quarters we ever inhabited – and the patterns always matched perfectly, all corners 'cut-in' like a pro!), collecting, visiting etc. But when we arrived at Ted's house the old man, although well into his 80s, was atop a house-high ladder with a paintbrush in his hand painting his guttering. On closer inspection, and having to wait patiently to speak to him when he had finished his task, dad couldn't help but notice that Ted was actually painting the inside of the gutters – work that no-one would ever, surely, see.

So, dad asked Ted why he was being so meticulous in his work for no apparent reason. Ted's reply has stayed with me for the rest of my life. A little smile lit his face and he pointed directly above us at a few brown house-sparrows flying in the blue sky above us. "See those birds?" he asked us. "They'll see their Lord before I do – and I don't want them telling Him that Ted Stevens was a shoddy workman!"

Now, while I cannot claim that anywhere close to all my own work has subsequently met Ted's exacting standards in all the interim decades, that simple lesson has always stayed with me and has challenged me on many an occasion when I have been tempted to offer a task anything less than my best – and it is indeed a great lesson for us all.

It was at Bargoed that I also have my first memories of specific Army events. There was the YP prize-giving when, one year, dad invited the legendary Welsh footballer John Charles to hand out the books. I had been told that he was a famous player but all I remember is this tall, imposing man and the fact he was 'very important'. This was before I began accumulating my now encyclopaedic knowledge of football or else I'm sure I'd have been considerably more thrilled to meet such a legend at the time! Back then I was probably more impressed with the free book!

This photograph shows the Young People of Bargoed corps with some of the band in June 1968. Uncle Trevor (Harry) is far left, mum the 2nd in uniform from the right at the back. I am in the centre of the front row of children in darker clothes and my sister Eira is 5 to my right on the end of the row. My cousins Janet and Graham are behind me to my left and there are several more that have remained friends throughout life there as well – such as the three Browning boys Robert, Ian and Adrian.

There was a good reason I remember Wednesdays: that was the day I didn't have to walk home from school but walked to the SA Hall instead because mum would always be found at the Home League meeting. The Home League was/is a Spiritual meeting held just for the ladies of the corps. One particular Wednesday I remember seeing all the tables being laid out with tea and cakes, cups, saucers and plates and there was my mum, with her back turned, leaning over one of the tables pouring a cuppa. She had her uniform on, complete with her bonnet, by the way…why should I ever not have thought that it was my mum?

Rather than give her a hug to let her know I was there I pulled back my hand and smacked her bottom! Only then did the Divisional Commander's wife, the special guest for that day's Home League Rally, turn around with the most indignant look a five year old boy could ever imagine and scare me half to death and back! I learned another lesson that day!!

I was allowed to join the singing company two years early at Bargoed. The leader was the band's euphonium player, Emlyn – son of the erstwhile Bandmaster Reg While. I can actually remember the first time I ever had a piece of printed music put in front of me and wondering what on earth it meant! Eventually, someone showed me that between all the wiggly, dotty lines I could read the words to sing. It was enough for then…deciphering the dotty hieroglyphics came later!

Also at Bargoed I remember becoming aware of the place of personal testimony in Army meetings for the first time. Dad used to try to include the opportunity for such participation and witness in his meetings whenever possible and I have strong memories from various corps of the testimony periods in his meetings. It was not only giving the opportunity to the congregation to take part that I think dad loved but also the chance to use some of the many great choruses found at the back of the song book that, otherwise, might have been overlooked (and are so sadly missed in the Army of today). That was how I became acquainted with the likes of 'I'm living on the mountain underneath a cloudless sky', 'My sins rose as high as the mountain', 'In the Army ranks are we', 'Gone, gone, gone, gone, all my sins are gone!' and many other examples that I still recall today. Through testimony periods I also learned to associate songs with people and I'm sure the Browning family will be delighted to learn that I have thought of them every time in over fifty years that I have sung the song 'A Wonderful Saviour is Jesus my Lord' for Mel Browning would always quote the chorus of that song every time he testified.

Much to the embarrassment of my corps officers on one occasion their 5 year old son rose to 'testify' in a meeting! For some reason unknown to me (although I had managed to pick up a few things at home that I shouldn't have already...as I shall explain below...) singing company practices had been cancelled for some weeks due to the circumstances of the leader. So I rose to my feet when the opportunity was given and asked when they were to restart! Not exactly what the testimony period was designed for, I know, but I suppose, in my infant ways, I was really just saying how much I enjoyed practicing music to sing for my Lord...so, I suppose, it was a testimony (of sorts) after all!

Talking of things I should not, perhaps, have heard: living with active Salvation Army officers did lead, on several occasions during my life as a child and even into adulthood later, to me overhearing some things that were obviously not intended for my ears. This, I would guess, is one of the 'responsibilities' of being an 'OK' – for, had I not realized from my earliest days the importance of a minister's 'confidence' I can only imagine the trouble I might have caused. I must confess that due to accidentally overheard conversations over the years between my parents, telephone calls and other meetings I did discover quite a few 'secrets' about people and situations in various corps that I am sure to this day others may not know.

Of course I would never even hint at the details here and the individuals concerned – mostly now long Promoted to their homes in Glory - have, in any case, had any long-past indiscretions forgiven and forgotten by a FAR higher authority than me! However, this is a 'hidden' part of life as an Officer's Kid that, I'm sure, many corps folk overlook. However small we may be, OKs have responsibilities too, and, as I've explained, these are often far greater than our tender years would have normally prepared us for.[1]

I started 'proper' school in Bargoed. From what I can recall I turned left out of our front door in Henry Street, turned right and then onto the great hill called Church Street. Somewhere at the bottom of this I turned left and found the school. (Internet maps now tell me that there were a few extra roads, twists and turns in the journey but St Gwladys

---

[1] On the one occasion as a VERY young boy of four I did repeat an overheard accusation against a soldier allegedly seen smoking in public –. I was so severely reprimanded I doubt I'd have ever dared do it again. So, it became a lesson learned by both myself and my parents – who had, I remember, actually SPELT their conversation only for their nosey little brainbox son to decipher it anyway! They never spelt messages to each other again either!

School still sits where it did back then). I'm sure I must have been 'walked' there by my mum at first but soon, having learned the route, I made the journey alone – there and back twice a day, for it was 'home for lunch' back then! Nobody had worries about 5 year old children walking to and from school on their own in the late 1960s – which is a very sad indictment of the world we are forced to live in just a generation or so later. Sometimes I walked back up Church Street with a school friend, David Harrhy, whose surname always puzzled me – I used to wonder if his parents couldn't spell properly not knowing, then, that he had the Irish version of our old, Welsh family name.

But apart from David I cannot remember any other classmates, except a boy called Anthony who had freckles, reddish hair and a permanently snotty nose. I did have two lovely teachers though and, coincidentally, both were called Mrs. Williams. Firstly there was 'old' Mrs Williams - a thin, kindly lady with grey/white hair and then I moved into 'young' Mrs Williams's class and 'young' Mrs Williams was plumper with black hair piled into a mini 'bee-hive' style. She wore lots of make-up, especially bright red lipstick, and I can vividly recall the day she taught us 'borrowing tens' subtraction!

Now, having lived with two of the hardest working Salvation Army officers I've ever known, it rather shames me to recall a story from one of my earliest parent's evenings. My dad used to read The Daily Telegraph. I must say that this was NOT, in any way at all, a reflection of his political leanings for I'm as sure as I ever could be that he voted nothing but Labour throughout his life but he LOVED the newspaper's sports coverage and, as I grew older, I too shared his joy in reading through beautifully written descriptions of the day's play at every county cricket ground (although especially Glamorgan's, of course!) savouring the prose of great writers like E.W. Swanton. To balance this, dad also used to buy the Daily Mirror, for both he and his father, Grandad Harry, were avid completists of the Daily Mirror Quizword. Both, I fondly recall, would fill in what they knew first of all and then look up missing answers in the Pears Cyclopaedia - dad always writing in biro but grandad with a pencil complete with wound rubber band on the other end to rub out any erroneous answers. Both men continued this 'habit' until only just before they died – keeping the brain active and still learning right up to the end – what an example!

Anyway, once more I digress (this book is rather like an endless Ronnie Corbett monologue…) back to the story! When I used to leave for school dad, having got down from the breakfast table ("what's one of those?" younger readers may ask!) would sit in his armchair for a few minutes (I'm sure it was just that!) and read the Telegraph. I'm sure he was not always home when I got back but, if he was, I suppose there was a fair chance he might have been having an afternoon cuppa and another browse. So, when asked in school one day "What does your father do for a job?" I couldn't answer miner, or postman, or doctor – I said "he reads the paper!" Of course, the teacher saved up this little anecdote for parent's evening and I'm not sure I ever quite lived it down. No wonder I was often referred to as a 'cheeky monkey'!

Chapter Eight – Officer or Construction Manager?

My dad, having 'done something' about the hall situation at Newport, his previous appointment, had little idea of what he had let himself in for. The Salvation Army is a very astute organization (or, at least, it was back then) and it soon got to know its 'horses for courses'. Ken Harry must have had a tick in a box somewhere at Headquarters for, from now on, and with very few exceptions, almost all of his corps appointments needed either major work on the SA Hall or quarters – or both!

You didn't have to look for too long at Bargoed SA hall to see the problem. The side wall to the left of the entrance was completely bowed! These days, I am 100% certain that the Health & Safety experts would condemn it immediately and the corps would have been left without a hall until it was remedied. However, the late 1960s was a different era and, doubtless, this problem had been getting progressively worse for decades and nothing done.

I can picture the wall now as I type – like the arc of a circle bending out and back in, from guttering to pavement. Something had to be done – and so it was. Things had to be shifted inside the hall so that the corps could continue to use the building for as long as possible during building work – so they were shifted – not by people you had to pay to do the job professionally, mind you – but by dad, his brother Trevor and some of the other men of the corps. With dad and Trevor one each end of the big, heavy wooden Penitent Form (a large bench used for prayer in Salvation Army meetings) a hitherto unknown further problem very soon revealed itself: underneath this old structure the floorboards were rotten. Trevor's foot went through the floor and he tore the tendons in his left ankle, causing him to be off work injured for the next 8 weeks!

Dad and Trevor replaced the floorboards themselves as well as the skirting boards and dado rails. Meanwhile, the corps continued to worship in the bits of the hall where there was floor and with polythene sheeting replacing the side wall for several months while construction workers replaced the bowed wall.

I have many other fond memories of times in that hall – perhaps my favourites were the 'Faggots and Peas' suppers regularly held there. Faggots and peas is a peculiar Welsh delicacy enjoyed in the valleys and a meal that has remained a regular family favourite even with my own children today. There was one particular butcher who lived in the little village of Ystrad Mynach, about half way between Bargoed and Caerphilly, who made the finest faggots in the world (well, no-one will ever convince me otherwise, anyway!) For the uninitiated, faggots are balls of minced pork and pork offal wrapped in caul (a thin layer of webbed fat from around the animal's internal organs) and roasted. For the communal meal these are reheated with gallons of gravy and lots of large tins of marrowfat processed peas. The tale from many years later of my mother's embarrassment when offering a late-evening supper of nice, hot faggots to two visiting Salvationist US servicemen will need no further explanation to the modern reader!

I loved going to Ystrad Mynach – some fields near the town still had green and grey, metal army Nissen huts left over from World War II that the farmers now used for storage – but it was the visit to the butcher that was always the highlight.

The undoubted highlight of the corps year at Bargoed, though, was The Rhymney Valley Festival. There was always a visiting band for the weekend and a big concert was held each year on the Saturday evening in the Central Hall. The two bands who came as guests to the Festival in the years we were at the corps were both to go on to play roles later in my life – and I was to serve as a bandsman at one of them for 26 years. They were Chalk Farm Band and Portsmouth Citadel Band.

Chalk Farm Band was always one of the most famous brass bands in the whole of Salvation Army history. Under the historic leadership of the great Bandmaster A.W. Punchard they had written whole chapters of army banding history and I was under no false illusions – even then - as to just how illustrious our guests were. To add to that, their young bandmaster, Michael Clack, was famous the army world over – for he was the man who played the grand organ in the Royal Albert Hall to such great effect at all Army events held in that wonderful building. Michael and his brother Peter had been teenage friends with my mother, so there was some family connection with the band too.

Michael stayed with our family in Henry Street that weekend and little did I know that, fourteen years later, he was to be my Vice-

Principal and euphonium teacher at Music College when I took my degree at Colchester Institute. By then, though, we had met many more times and I had developed enormous respect for a man who is still today one of the finest musicians I have ever met. Certainly he is one of the three best brass band conductors whose batons I have had the privilege of playing under with both the college band and, on just one occasion, as a guest 2nd trombone player on a radio broadcast with Chalk Farm Band themselves.

Chalk Farm Band was subsequently invited to almost every corps my parents ever officered after that weekend. I can distinctly recall visits to Camborne (though under the leadership of Ray Farr by then), Torquay, Tunstall and Felixstowe…but there were, most probably, others too. One little aside to that Rhymney Valley Festival was only discovered a short time ago when I found some photographs of the visit. In recent years I have become an 'afficionado' of TV cooking programmes and, as a result, I have taught myself to cook to what I hope is an acceptable standard [2] The bottom 2nd cornet player that weekend in Bargoed was none other than the now famous TV chef Brian Turner during the time he spent at the corps and it is a time in his life that Brian still talks about very fondly on the many occasions he has been interviewed about it in recent years.

[2] My two older sons cook too; Lewis having learned from me and with me through the TV and my eldest, Morgan, works as a chef.

The other band that came to the Rhymney Valley Festival during our stay was Portsmouth Citadel Band – then under the leadership of one of my other 'top three' band trainers and conductors, the late BM Harold Nobes[3]. It was 1968 as well…and any bandsman who has played in any version of 'PCB' since then will know just how heavily lies the shadow cast by the famous '68 Band'! And what a band they were! I thank God that I got to know so many of them personally later but, at the time, I

[3] The third 'giant' in my list is Dr Robert Childs under whom I was privileged to play with Woodfalls (non-SA) band. He made ANY music live but playing the simple hymn tune Aberystwyth at the start of a secular band rehearsal will always remain both one of my all-time musical highlights AND an intensely Spiritual moment as well.

remember being impressed by their power and precision, their deportment and their keen Salvationism.

I also knew that, that weekend, they had played one very special piece. While I remember the 'big' piece being played and the reverent, 'Holy' hush that descended on the concert hall I cannot say honestly that I sat enraptured by every note - but I know for a fact that my father did.: for that piece was Eric Ball's 'Resurgam'.

In my own, and many other peoples' opinion 'Resurgam' is not just the best brass band piece ever composed but one of the best pieces of music ever…in any era or genre. It was, much later, to be one of the last pieces I ever played with Portsmouth Citadel Band back in 2010 when my 26 years with the band came to an end. How fitting that that should be the case when I had first become aware of the beauty of brass band music all those years before through that very same piece, and played, no less, by the very same band.

There are a few other people I remember from Bargoed – Gladys and Edna were two older ladies who attended the corps, then there was the friendly couple over the road from us in Henry Street (she was called Edith), to whose house we were always instructed to go after school if mum and dad had been called out on 'army duty'. This caused a bit of a problem on one occasion, I'm often reminded…

You may recall that in the earlier chapters on Clapham I had started having a very strange, recurring dream (or nightmare might be a better word). In it, everyone I knew was descending one of those big, old wooden escalators that used to be seen on the London Underground, standing in single file with their mouths all open wide, teeth removed and a big, unshelled walnut in their mouths! (I said it was bizarre!) I can still see the people on that escalator in my mind's eye right now being swallowed into the bowels of the earth via the slowly moving staircase…

For this reason I developed one of the very few 'phobias' I ever had in my life – the fear of seeing people I knew and loved without their teeth in. Even today it gives me a shiver! I have no idea if our friendly neighbour, Edith Jones, had just returned from a serious visit to her dentist or whether she just had sore gums that prevented her wearing her dentures on that particular day but I'm told that on that day, finding this lovely, kind lady with a gaping void where her teeth usually sat, I point blank refused to enter her house and I became rather upset. I actually have a vague recollection of the event – such must have been the associated trauma to my young mind! To this day if I see someone without their teeth in, or a footballer who takes his teeth out to play (I never liked Joe Jordan or Iwan Roberts!) it makes me feel uncomfortable…how on EARTH was I ever to once consider dentistry as a career choice?

There is only one other story that I'd like to share from Bargoed and that is one that can teach us two lessons in life – the first being to always listen to advice when offered and the other that 'pride goes before a fall'…and maybe point to the possibility of one's subsequent 'rise again' afterwards as well! One of the gentlemen in the corps was a keen amateur gardener and had planted his borders with the 'flowers' he had hoped would flourish and bring colour to his garden later in the year.

When the seedlings began to sprout some time later a passer-by, seeing him weeding one day, asked him why he had planted turnips in his flower borders. Eric laughed and just shrugged off the question as a joke…until no flowers appeared on the plants! However, Mr. Roberts did win the prize for best turnips in the town's garden show a few months later!

St David's Day 1968 at Bargoed Infants- the girls wore the traditional Welsh costumes and the boys sported daffodils – I'm the one with the silly smile and the XXXL flower!

Chapter Nine – 'Harry the Trom'

Somewhere in my possession I have a case full of reel-to-reel tapes. They will, no doubt hold a great deal of long-forgotten and long-lost things if and when I ever get around to listening to them! I do remember going through them once, when I had a suitable tape recorder in my possession some years ago; some things that I was asked to look out for by my parents I did manage to find – but others, much wanted by both them and me, were not. Although mum and dad are no longer with us I'd still be very interested in hearing them.

Apparently, dad used to have a recorder many, many years ago that 'doubled' the amount of time a tape reel could hold by recording four separate mono tracks instead of two stereo ones. That might explain why I had some difficulties finding the said 'lost items', for on those tapes – somewhere – I was assured are two recordings of my dad playing trombone solos and, just maybe, one day I will look and actually find them. But, as yet, they exist only in legend and my hopes…

Dad learned to play a brass instrument as a young lad at Cardiff Stuart Hall Corps. I recently came across this photograph of him and the other young bandsmen from Stuart Hall in their festival tunics, including dad and his brothers Trevor and Owen. Peter, dad's youngest brother, also played with the band but a little while later.

The 1940s when dad learned to play an instrument was, of course, a very different era from the world in which we live today and for young Ken to be taught by a kindly, Christian gentleman - complete with steel knitting needle to bring down on errant valve-pressing fingers – might not quite be as acceptable in 2025 as it was in that bygone age!

I grew up hearing about the great Erik Leidzen quote in which he asserted that he would 'forgive any bandsman for playing a wrong note – once - but let him make the same mistake again and it would be no longer a mistake at all, but gross negligence! I have to say that Ken Harry never had anything but the utmost respect and love for Ernie Jones (below, with dad) who was the man who taught him to play and he was both truly, and 'painfully', aware that the 'knitting needle approach' had worked for him and his knuckles!

Despite this (and the fact dad was a competent enough instrumentalist on valve instruments) it was his love of the trombone that captured his heart. He had his 'trombone idols' in Arthur Rolls, Maisie Ringham etc. whom he listened to on his SA 78rpm records and, later in life, he was equally able to appreciate the talents of modern players such as Don Lusher, Andrew Justice and others– but, by spending most of his working life as a Salvation Army officer, dad sacrificed the opportunity to ever develop his trombone playing fully.

A high-ranking SA 'music department' Officer once told dad that, as a young officer, a letter appointing him to the International Staff Band was actually written – only for the Field Secretary of the day to suddenly require dad's skills elsewhere – and that, as they say, was that. He often told me he would have gladly 'carried the lamp' for the Staff Band if it had meant he could have been involved with them in some way.

The picture below shows dad playing a solo on his 'pea-shooter' trombone – an SP&S instrument that he owned for years and kept in what seemed a very tiny, brown leather case.

Dad started collecting those Regal Zonophone label, Salvation Army Band 78rpm records that were made by the ISB, SP&S Band, Tottenham Citadel and many other Army bands long before he ever left home (first made in 1928 – then through to 1957) and he listened to these records throughout his life. Tales were told to me fondly about how he could identify any of the records from hearing just one note (a game he, apparently, loved to play as a cadet). I remember him piling these brittle, black discs on the 'rest' spindle of his old gramophone and hearing them 'plop' down one on top of the other as he listened to the scratchy, crackle and hiss they produced amongst the notes that were, nonetheless, recognizable as 'music'!

Dad always wanted the records to be put onto cassettes so he could listen while in the car but such gramophones that still had the capability of playing 78s never had the 'phono out' plugs necessary for this task – so, short of placing a tape recorder in front of the gramophone and keeping quiet while they played, it was never possible for him to achieve this.

Since his Promotion to Glory in 2002, though, I have developed the skills to 'clean up' the sound of such 78s with computers and have done this with the collection of 78s that he left behind – which, in the end, was almost a full collection – and I enjoyed listening to them myself until rather reluctantly passing them on to someone else to care for recently. Occasionally, though, I use the recordings on my podcast "Going to the Army!" which has many thousands of listeners a month from all around the world. I am rather sorry that dad, though, never had the chance to hear the 78s like I can today – all cleaned up and crackle-free!

I can remember dad playing just about every instrument in the band at the various corps we spent time at – he really didn't enjoy playing the cornet (and it wasn't good for his ears/hearing problems) but he obliged when necessary (e.g. at Heckmondwike). He played euphonium at Camborne, 2nd baritone in Portsmouth Citadel, Eb bass – anywhere – when there was no-one else who could! But he always loved his trombone. The highlight of the year for him for very many years was 'Butlins Week' – the Army's 'Holiday Plus Fellowship' at Bognor Regis (occasionally Skegness) and dad had his seat on the end of the trombone section reserved for him every year by his friends Norman Bearcroft and Trevor Davis!

With the 'Butlins Citadel Band' dad had the opportunity to play solos in band pieces – particularly memorable was his playing of the tune 'Beautiful Christ' in Norman Bearcroft's selection 'Sing Along With the Band' and the 'banter' he often shared with perennial Butlins host Norman was often funny and entertaining.

One of my personal treasures is a DVD I made of a BBC 'Songs of Praise' episode from Butlins, Skegness in which dad can be seen in his 'rightful place' on the end of a line of what was probably 30 trombonists at that time.

In the photograph below, from a Salvation Army magazine, dad can be seen 'on the march' with the 'Butlins Citadel Band'.

A bandsmen's holiday: Army instrumentalists relax in civvies

Dad was also a collector of LPs, cassettes and even reel-to-reel recordings – some that he made himself. The undoubted highlight from amongst them is a recording dad made from the gallery in the old Newcastle City Temple Hall when the ISB visited in 1957. As far as I am aware no other recordings exist of Jos Walford playing 'The Ransomed Host' or Arthur Rolls playing Leidzen's 'Concertino for Band

and Trombone' and both of these are on the tape. Happily dad was able to enjoy this transfer for several years before he 'moved upstairs'.

Talking about Newcastle dad used to talk very fondly of his time there as Youth Officer when he had the opportunity to play regularly with the corps band under the leadership of Arthur Bristow. Somewhere on the said tapes he was always adamant was a recording of dad as soloist with the Temple Band playing Brindley Boon's solo 'Count Your Blessings'. Dad used to joke with Brindley that the solo had been written for him and that he was waiting for the 'follow-up' – a standing joke between them that was repeated whenever they met later in life. I would SO love to find that recording one day but it has never 'come to light' despite much searching and the only solo I ever recall hearing dad play was 'Happy am I' with piano accompaniment.

There is also said to be another trombone solo on those tapes – a home-made one that dad recorded and sent to my mother while courting – although I'm sure the title 'Lovest Thou Me' might have had its original intent and meaning somewhat 'bent' on that occasion!

Two other recordings I have yet to find on those tapes involve my sister Eira and I talking and singing into a microphone (in fact I can clearly remember both recordings being made). Although the recordings were, I was always told, recorded barely six months apart they demonstrate another of the changes that 'OK's go through as they follow their parents' Marching Orders around the world...

One final, great adventure for me during our time in Bargoed was the opportunity to take part in the Divisional production of the musical 'Take Over Bid'. The musical was the first of many such works written and composed by a pair of Salvation Army officers – John Gowans (words) and John Larsson (music). They had been asked to write a musical for 1967 which had been designated 'Youth Year' in The Salvation Army. If I'm correct in my memory it was future British Commissioner Denis Hunter whose brainchild the venture was while in his role as National Youth Secretary.

John Gowans was a good family friend of ours, having been a Sergeant for dad's year in the Training College and his presence was always a massive influence in my life. I have many recollections of hearing him preach

– always with such infectious passion and challenge! Many, many years later – when I was a parent myself – my two older sons (probably about 6 and 4 years old) came home from a Divisional Congress he had led and were repeating phrases from his sermons as they shared their night-time bath together:

"No – we never, never, never will give in! No we won't – MIND YOU DON'T!"

"You've got to have a dream! If you don't have a dream, how are you going to have a dream COME TRUE?"

Precious moments indeed from my own parenting. Great preaching crosses generations – just as Commissioner Mingay's had done for me all those years before!

But John G's family friendship with us played no part in my getting the role of 'Millions' in the production! That, so I'm told, happened as a result of the previous year's Officer's Children Party! The affair, apparently, was a fancy dress party and, although other OK's had come in costume, only one stepped forward to take part in the 'talent show'. Dressed in a powder blue, silk two-piece of blouson and pantaloons I had gone to the party as 'Little Boy Blue'. I SO seriously doubt that this was my choice (thanks mum!)

Whatever the reasoning – it happened, and I duly stepped forward in the shiny suit (which I CAN remember) to sing:

"Little Boy Blue, Come blow your horn,

There's sheep in the meadow, the cow's in the corn"

complete with my little horn, on a ribbon, around my neck!

Because no other 'OK' came forward to take part it seems I won by default and was, consequently, put forward by the Divisional Commander to take the part of 'Millions'.

'Millions' refers not to the name of a character in the cast of 'Take Over Bid' but to my most memorable line. There is a song that the three children had to sing in the show – one that has gone on to be a favourite right up to the present day and is currently in the SA songbook – 'Hundreds and Thousands'.

The last verse of the four we sang reads:

There are hundreds of children.

Thousands! MILLIONS!

And yet their names are written in God's memory.

There are hundreds and thousands, millions of children.

And God knows every one – and God knows ME!

Bearing in mind that I couldn't have been more than 5 years old I can vividly remember meeting my two 'sisters' for the first time in Ivor and Janette Bosanko's front room for the first rehearsal.

One of the girls was Bev Jones, daughter of Ernie who – many years before – had taught my dad to play an instrument, complete with the afore-mentioned steel knitting needle!

Full rehearsals followed, invariably at Cardiff Canton SA and I can clearly remember (again!) the show taking shape. I was captivated by seeing people I knew as young pretending to be much older, long-bearded stalwarts of the Corps census board! I marvelled at the manual dexterity of Leslie Fish during the song 'Break Down the Bad, Build Up the Good' as his hand gymnastics illuminated a song that became one of my favourites from the show. I can even remember the 'Spiritual moment' in the Youth Club during which one of the young people, Chris (played by Haydn Whitcombe) realised the futility of trying to turn the Army into something different without ever considering putting God at the centre – the character's despair getting through to me in another clear lesson in my own Christian development.

You won't be surprised that, by the time of the performances, I knew every word of every song – and Ivor Bosanko kindly asked me to be on stage with the whole cast for all of the Finale rather than just the part that the children were meant to be present for so I could get a bit more 'stage time'. What a surprise to anyone who has ever known me since!

I have met many of the cast since again, of course, online or in person– but have always been rather surprised that they no longer look the same as I remembered them from 1968! I guess I've changed too!

I've almost always been in touch with Malcolm Young whose dad, Les, was later BM at Canton. I remember the real-life trauma Haydn Whitcombe experienced as his young wife Althea – a beautiful auburn-haired lady (who had also been in the cast) – died from cancer. One of the chorus members even became my Corps Officer many years later!

It was a great experience for a young lad – and it came about all because of Little Boy Blue!

SOUTH WALES DIVISION

presents

Take Over Bid

CAST

John	Derek Lucas
Julie	Eleanor Harris
Brains	David Roberts
Stella	Susan Osborne
George	David Murray
Gladys	Lynne Brill
Ethel	Janet Hayman
Herbert	Robert Hayman
Archibald	Richard Gillmore
Corps Cadet Guardian	Barbara Lyons
Home League Secretary	Althea Whitcombe
Treasurer	David Holton
The Major	Andries Gronenburg
Children	Susan Davies
	Beverley Jones
	Marc Harry
Chris	Hadyn Whitcombe
Harry	Alan Hardwicke
Darby	Brinley Sutton
Joan	Kay Ford
Tony	Gordon Weaver
Janet	Hilary Spear
Teenager	Gareth Jones

Girls : Susan Andrews, Judith Bowers, Marjorie Bowers, Cynthia Beaven, Marion Davies, Ann Dunstan, Pamela Griffin, Christine Hawkins, Irene Hawkins, Beverley Jones, Jennifer Jones, Christine Turk.

Boys : Colin Davies, Leslie Fish, Paul Fish, Peter Gittins, Clive Griffin, Graham Jones, Christopher Lee, Cedric Morgan, John Vallely, Colin Weaver, Anthony Yelland, Malcolm Young.

PART 1.

Sequence 1. "Hall Scene."
Sequence 2. "Local Officers' Meeting."
Sequence 3. "Street Scene."
Sequence 4. "Coffee Club Scene."

PART 2.

Sequence 1. "Hall Scene."
Sequence 2. "Finale."

ORCHESTRA

Organ—Janette Bosanko. Piano—June Murray.
Trumpets—Glyn Bosanko, Leslie Young.
Euphonium—Chris Mallet. Bass—Barry Gelatly.
Percussion—Robert Humphries.

BAND

Canton Citadel.

SUPPORTING CHORUS

The voices of Abercarn, Canton Citadel, Roath Temple and Newport Mairdee Songsters.

MUSICAL DIRECTOR : Ivor Bosanko.

DECOR : Ian Davies.

PRODUCTION : Frank J. Shepherd.

(Sorry it's sideways but I so wanted to include the programme in readable form. There are so many names and families here familiar throughout my life.)

89

Chapter Ten – Ferrybridge and Knottingley

Shortly before we left Bargoed the recording I mentioned at the end of the last chapter was made of me reading a poem from a book. The poem I recited, in the broadest of Welsh valleys accents, was 'Amelia Jane and her sooooper delicious birthday cake.' I was never to be able to live it down – reminded at every available opportunity for the next decade or more. My sister Eira, of course, despite having been born in London, spoke in a similar fashion.

Yet a few short months later a second family recording has her reading,

"T' purple 'eaded marntin, t'river runnin' bah. The soonset and t'mornin' that brahtens oop the skah."

For we had left the Welsh valleys behind after four years in my homeland and upped sticks to the West Riding of Yorkshire. The nearest most people get to Ferrybridge were the enormous cooling towers that sat beside the A1 near to where it crossed the M62. It's nearest and better known towns are Castleford and Featherstone – both deep-seated rugby league municipalities – and Pontefract, home of a racecourse and the British home of liquorice sweets. Trips to Pontefract inevitably ended with a bag of Pontefract Cakes to bring home and, often, some sticks of Coltsfoot Rock too, which were a favourite of mum's.

I remember very little about my school in Ferrybridge apart from the fact my teacher was called Mrs. Lockhead. I played football for the school team who wore the 'Everton' kit of blue shirts – but mine was always my treasured Cardiff City shirt, of course! I remember falling in the playground one day and embedding three large stones in my left knee – the traffic light arrangement of scars this left still adorn my left patella today – but, with those exceptions, the whole year at school is a rare 'blank' in my usually retentive mind.

I remember a little more about the Salvation Army Corps, of course. I started to learn a brass instrument properly for the first time under the kind and patient eye and ear of YPBL Ron Taylor, whose wife Rita, was also the Singing Company Leader. I still have the remnants of that very first manuscript book in which Ron had written out the notes of 'Drink to me Only' ('Behold the Saviour' in the Army tune book!) and had circled the 'C' in red biro with the words 'high note' in capital letters. Ron became another 'faith hero' to me and we stayed in touch for many years. Many years later I wrote a letter to the SA publication 'The Musician' in which I thanked him and others who had so selflessly been willing to help me on my early musical journey. My mum and Ron's widow continued to write and telephone each other until Rita was Promoted to Glory.

There were other boys in the corps, older than I, who I remember also developing their skills on brass instruments: the flame haired Ian Gott (son of CSM Joe Gott) was a fine cornettist while two other boys (one of whom was the BM's son, Andre Heath) frequently featured on corps programmes as duettists. Another boy, Jamie Dunn, played the tenor horn and I used to listen with admiration as he played

Air Varie (theme with variation) solos like 'Shepherd of Israel' with all their fast notes.

These were all inspirations to me as a young boy, not yet seven years old, just setting out in the world of music and I thank God for the likes of Ron who taught me those first lessons and the other boys who I watched, open-mouthed, and longed to emulate. I never made it to Ron's YP Band at that time but, as I said above, I recall a few other players in the young people's ensemble were good soloists.

Those early lessons may not have produced any kind of 'finished article' in me but I am very aware that they played their part in my development as a musician. I have since learned just how much patience is needed when trying to help beginners: and, therefore, YPBL Ron Taylor is a man I will always be grateful for and I still treasure the note I received in reply to my letter from his widow Rita in response to that letter in 'The Musician'.

The corps bandmaster, George Heath, was a well-known Army musician who had had pieces published in the band journals (for example the March – Knottingley as well as the very Air Varie I mentioned Jamie playing, above).

Although Knottingley could not even then have been described as a large corps, there was a healthy band and songster brigade in the corps in 1969 and a thriving YP corps, that is pictured below at the Harvest Festival. (In the photograph I am 2nd from the right on the front row; S/coy Leader Rita Taylor is on the left next to my mum. On the right in Indian costume is our friend Adam McCaig who was mentioned in a previous chapter.)

Three things happened of real significance during the time we spent at Knottingley Corps. One was personal: my parents discovered that my youngest sister was 'on the way' and the other two had to do with...yes, you guessed it...property!

For the first nine or ten months we were in this appointment the property we lived in was a council house some miles from the SA Hall in Ferrybridge, at the end of a close called Vale Head Mount. While the house was quite spacious I recall it had an extremely overgrown back garden that my sister and I could explore like 'mini-Attenboroughs' in our very own jungle!

More often, though, I remember the trees at the closed off end of the close being a far more fun place to play and we children spent quite some time playing there with the other youngsters in the locality. However, being a council property the house, of course, did not belong to the corps which had never 'owned' its own quarters at that time.

Talking about that garden, by the way, I remember two rather sinister looking utensils arriving at the house one day that were intended to help with its renovation – a massive farmer's scythe and a smaller sickle. I remember little about the said renovation with the exception of jumping into the car with dad and rushing my mother to the hospital for urgent stitches in a wound the sickle had caused!

However, I digress (again!)… In those days it was 'usual' for Salvation Army officers to stay in the same appointment for two years – very few stayed for three or four and longer than that was almost unheard of. Some of dad's early appointments as a single officer were better measured in months than years and it was to be another decade before the Harry family ever entered a third year in the same place. As it transpired, Knottingley was to be our home for only one year. My parents were told that, if they moved quarters to a property nearer the hall (in Knottingley itself) in the spring of 1970 then 'not to bother to unpack' and they would be moved to a new appointment in the May. The council duly found us such a property, arranged an exchange and, in due course, we moved to Knottingley town itself from Ferrybridge – and, thus, half the 'property work was soon a 'fait accompli' for my dad, the Army's Mr Fix-It at the time!

The larger job was, once again, the hall itself. It was one of those post war buildings erected with brick base and wooden walls – dad had had a very similar hall earlier in his officership in Ramsey, on the Isle of Man. Problem was, though, in Knottingley the wood on the outside of the hall needed replacing and so, once again, this necessitated major work on a building where dad was the Commanding Officer.

Although even this, at face value, appeared to be 'routine' work; the building, having been constructed with wood, could not have been expected to last for ever – so architect plans were drawn up, the contract awarded and the work began. I can recall the familiar feeling of a building being surrounded (once more!) by scaffolding and tarpaulins, the meetings continuing each Sunday with different walls missing all of the time. I'm sure that 'health and safety' would never allow this today (we were, effectively, worshipping in a building site) but no-one seemed to worry about such things in 1969!

Both the outer and inner wood was to be replaced in the hall, the outside with beautiful, best quality cedar and the inside with a lesser wood but still of good specifications.

Dad had been trained as a pattern-maker before his officership and he 'knew his wood', as one might say. He literally rejoiced in the quality of the cedar wood – I guess different things please different ones of us in different ways all the time – and all seemed to be progressing well.

Then one day, as the replacement wood panelling inside the hall was progressing, dad became rather worried. He suspected that the new panels were being fixed to the old, existing wooden framework and he tried to point this out to the foreman. Apparently, it uncovered some considerable problems with the work resulting in a real 'can of worms' being opened…not only had the old framework been retained, as dad had suspected, but further inspection found that this older wood was completely full of dry rot.

Whether or not there was some sort of 'cost-cutting' going on or other kind of shenanigans it is not my place here to speculate about – but, had dad not discovered the problem, the likely result would have been that that the whole job would have needed doing again just a few, short years later.

I'm delighted to say that the same building is still standing 55 years later…so dad must have done something right!

The refurbished hall was opened by the British Commissioner Albert Mingay, pictured below with dad and the Divisional Commander of the Central and West Yorkshire Division at the time Major Joe Evans, at the ceremony and rededication.

This was the first of several associations that these two fine, Christian gentlemen were to have with our family. Commissioner Mingay took a special interest in me personally and 'specialled' for dad at several appointments in the years ahead with his wife, who I remember had a beautiful singing voice. He wanted very much to swear me in as a senior soldier when the time came but, sadly, Mrs Mingay had entered into failing health by then and he was unable to fulfil that wish by the time 1976 arrived.

At the time of Knottingley, however, I had merely reached a tender 7 years of age and, so, I was made a Junior Soldier there.

Although I can remember the actual enrolment ceremony, conducted by my dad. I'm afraid I can recall very little about my first 6 months or so as a JS…and even less about my time in the singing company at that time, I can't recall the street map of either Ferrybridge or Knottingley (strange, as I CAN remember how to get from A to B in Bargoed) and, in the 46 years since I left I have only ever returned twice; once with my parents in the early 1980s when they conducted a Corps Anniversary weekend (I recall playing some euphonium solos on that occasion).

I then went back to Knottingley just a few years ago with Lincoln Band and Songsters to do a Saturday Evening festival and it was good to see that hall again – and several people I remembered, including BM George Heath. As the band and songsters returned to Lincoln I stayed in Knottingley to lead the Sunday meetings on that occasion.

It was lovely to meet some old friends again, most notably BM Heath, then in his 90s (now PTG) and still playing with the band (below).

Chapter Eleven – Heckmondwike

It's quite fair to say the 'new' house we moved into for just a few months, in Knottingley, never really felt like home at all. Rooms and corridors stayed crammed with boxes and although I'm sure we didn't really live out of suitcases it did feel a bit like that. It must have come as a bit of a relief, then, when May arrived and we finally got to complete our 'move' just 21 miles due West along what is now the M62.

NEW ARMY OFFICERS ARRIVE

YOUTH WORK will play an important part in the duties of the new Commanding Officers of the Heckmondwike Salvation Army Corps, Captain and Mrs. Kenneth Harry, who arrived in the town last Thursday.

The officers — who replace Major and Mrs. Leslie Petrie who have taken charge of the Bradford Great Horton Corps after two-and-a-half years in Heckmondwike—are also looking forward to working with the older Army members.

Captain and Mrs. Harry have come from the Knottingley Corps where they had been in charge for 12 months. Previously they have been in several parts of the country including South Wales, London, the Isle of Man and Liverpool.

Captain Harry (39), was born in Cardiff. For more than five years he was a full-time youth officer with the Salvation Army.

His wife, Margaret, who is 30, was born in Hastings. They have two children—Marc (7) and Eira (6).

Captain Harry stressed that they intended the various organisations within the Army would continue in their present form.

■ Our picture shows the new Officers with their two children after arriving in Heckmondwike.

Heckmondwike was a small town then - just a mile square – and it was still dominated by woollen mills and carpet manufacture. The Salvation Army Hall was on the site of an old military Army barracks, opposite the town park and just a short distance from the main town square. The officer's quarters was a flat above the actual SA hall – Barrack House in Barracks Street and my new 'back garden' consisted of a tarmac veranda above the band and songster rooms that was reached by going out of our kitchen door – this playground supplemented by a massive patch of waste ground between the hall itself and the 'hut' – an old wooden building that served as the YP Hall.

That patch of ground served as the corps car park, of course –

but, to me, it was my own personal Wembley Stadium! Half the size of a full football pitch I had enough room to kick my 'Bobby Moore Special' plastic football all day long, long summer day after long summer day! My 'goal' was a rugged, concrete wall – 40 ft high – that separated our 'land' from a massive, smoky carpet factory. Even I

couldn't lose my ball over a wall that high, although I did burst it on a nail!

My sister, Eira, was less keen on football (both then and still now!) and she would only play 'three and in' on the veranda. ('Three and in' was the popular game in our school playgrounds then – it was every man for himself, although we DID pass and set each other up and, when once of us reached 3 goals it became their 'turn' to go in goal.) I fondly recall Eira and I playing 'three and in' up on the veranda for many hours – and yes it was extremely irritating when the ball went over the edge. The veranda perimeter fence was only a couple of feet or so high…health and safety of the modern age would not have been very impressed, I'm sure, and every time we lost the ball over the edge it was: through the kitchen, into the hallway, out the door, down the concrete steps, round the path to 'Wembley Stadium', find the ball and back up the stairs again 'til the next time!

But Eira was crafty…while I was out ball-fetching (it was always me – but rightly so, I guess, seeing as I was usually the one who kicked the ball over the edge!) she would enact a quick substitution! When I returned she had gone inside and her replacement 'goalkeeper' had become her friendly, orange Spacehopper toy…and, if I complained, she would explain that, actually, I was better off as "the Spacehopper is a better goalie than me!" Oh, the trials of being a football-mad big brother to a girl!

A bit more, then, about our location: Barracks Street was a muddy, no tarmac road with a corner sweet shop at the end and, between that and the gates of the SA was a car showroom – not, alas, for Rolls-Royce automobiles but one for 3 wheel Reliant Robins and those pale blue 'invalid carriages' that were given to disabled drivers before today's infinitely better Motability scheme.

Turn left at the end of the street and you would be in the town square with its lawns, gardens and benches inside black, iron railings. Turn right and you'd be walking past another black, imposing woollen mill. There were windows at pavement level, through which we could see workers about their tasks while on our way to and from school each day. Another more open-plan factory area was next and it was here that I remember noticing, for the first time, the larger than usual numbers of Asian workers about their business. I was particularly fascinated by one Pakistani gentleman who had bright orange hair and beard – he used to drive a forklift truck around the site and must have often wondered who the snotty-nosed kid was who stared at him so often!

Further up the hill was a petrol station (Gulf) and then some streets, another sweet shop and then the turning to our school – Millbridge Upper for me and the infants for Eira, just outside of Heckmondwike, as it happened, into the next town/village of Liversedge.

Once again it was: walk to school, home for lunch and back to school followed by another walk home afterwards – no wonder children were fitter in those days! One of the streets around the school I always found fascinating. Keir Hardie Close had a building on it called Keir Hardie Hall. Somehow, it seemed very important yet I had absolutely no idea at the time that the esteemed gentleman the road and hall were named after was such a famous and important man – the first ever Labour MP, no less! The close is just one of some 40 streets in the UK named after him.

Heckmondwike Salvation Army was a lovely corps, thriving at that time with a band of well over 20, a similarly sized songster brigade and a large YP corps with an excellent singing company under the leadership of Singing Company Leader Linda Thompson – complete with her very special 'Three Musketeers'.

It was a new privilege for me to be able to lie in bed on a Tuesday evening and listen to the band practicing across the way in the hut or below my bedroom in the main hall. It was this band, therefore, that I first heard play marches like 'California' and 'Minneapolis IV', suites like 'Happiness and Harmony' and sing band songs such as 'It Took a Miracle' and 'Say there, Listen to Me!' – a song that I've loved but have never heard sung since, as it happens! Dad, as always, played with the band but, the trombone section being full at the time, he helped 'Hecky Band' on cornet, which always seemed strange to me but was typical of dad to simply want to be of use in whatever way he could.

As for me at Heckmondwike, for the first time in my life as an Officer's Kid, I was able to establish real friendships with the other lads in the corps. There were 5 of us lads in total: myself, Steven Lister, Glen Tillotson and two brothers – Mark and Ian Walker – but Steven, Glen and myself became inseparable buddies – 'The Three Musketeers' as Linda called us.

In the photo above, from left to right the boys are Mark, Steven, Ian, me and Glen is over on the right. We wore the old red Army Jerseys with short trousers, the girls scarlet red cardigans with white blouses, ties and singing company hats. As for the adults, S/Coy Ldr Linda Thompson is on the left next to her assistant and pianist Helen Foster, then my mum and, on the right Valerie Cost and Jean Hirst. Eira is in the front row, centre position, directly beneath the SA crest.

There was no YP Band at the time but all five of us boys were learning to play under the kind tutelage of the corps Bandmaster George

Brooke. George was, to me, the epitome of the 'gentle giant'. Standing a very imposing 6ft 4 or 5 he cut a most imposing figure – a natural authoritarian, well-suited to his 'day job' position of a headmaster. Yet I'm convinced I never heard George raise his voice. He patiently taught the 4 of us who played the cornet (only Ian Walker, the youngest of our number) played anything larger – a baritone – and George *(pictured below)* even wrote us some pieces that we could feature on Singing Company programmes.

The one I particularly remember featured two army choruses, "In the church they play the organ, In the Army bang the drum. All the lassies play their tambourines and the band goes 'Om pop pom, tiddly om pom pom!'" This was followed by "A Woman came to fill her water pot – down at the bottom of the well!" It was Ian, of course, who always raised a laugh from the congregations by playing the descending C scale on those final words. Happy memories indeed there, of some of my earliest brass playing exploits. Who knew back then that I would play 'Ransomed' and 'Song of the Brother' at twelve, record solos on many CDs and records as well as perform euphonium solos all over the UK, Germany, Holland, Switzerland, France, Norway and as far away as California! Small beginnings!

On Sunday mornings the young learners band were not allowed to sit and play with the senior band but we eventually sat on the front row in front of the platform and joined in the playing of the opening song. We used to really look forward to this and not least because Steven's dad Peter Lister would 'look after us', making sure we had the right tune and behaved, at least reasonably, well!

George Brooke was a single man who seemed to be destined to remain a bachelor despite his geniality and rather engaging personality (I happen to know he was one of just a few gentlemen who could make my mum swoon!) but he eventually met, fell in love with and married a young lady who was a Salvation Army officer and they became the proud parents of triplet sons!

We stayed in touch with George and his family for many years until his sudden and tragic death from a heart attack. He is pictured below, with his family visiting us in a later appointment in Bedlington, about 10 years after we first met.

The Heckmondwike Songsters rehearsed on Thursday evenings under the leadership of SL Ron Cost and some of the other things I was aware of happened in the corps by then included Home League and Over 60s and a 'Knitter's Fellowship' where ladies would knit and chat while the men had band practice (I should say that there WERE ladies in Heckmondwike Band at the time so this was NOT a sexist thing...and I'm sure men would have been just as welcome at the knitter's group!)

Just three months after we moved to Heckmondwike mum gave birth to my youngest sister, Ruth. Ruth (below) was born in Staincliffe Hospital, Dewsbury – and our Harry family was now complete...but Ruth came at a price. Mum became very ill around the time of Ruth's birth and was eventually diagnosed as suffering from gallstones. Whether it was the pain or the stress of looking after me as well I don't know but mum's hair lost all its colour within a matter of months and she became the 'pure white' of her own mother within about a year, despite being only 30 years old. Mum had been looking forward so much to having a new-born baby around the house again (there was a 6½ year gap between Eira and Ruth but mum was so unwell she couldn't look after Ruth for some time after her birth.

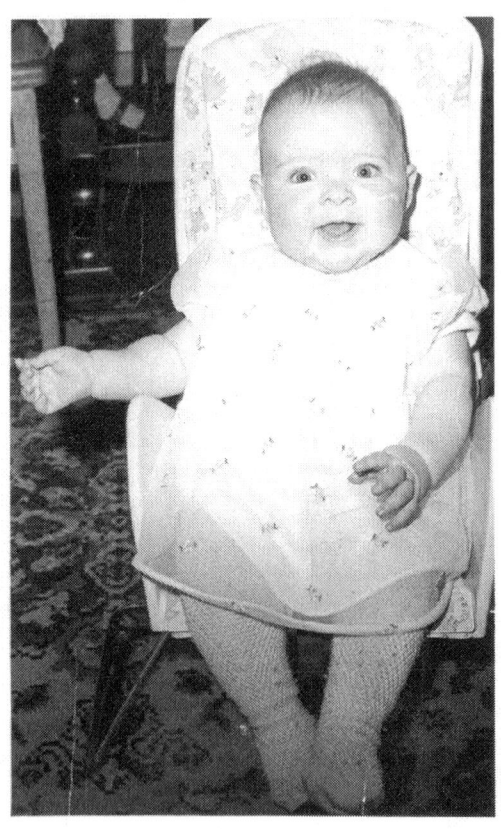

Very soon after bringing the baby home from hospital mum was bathing Ruth when she was overcome with a pain so severe and acute she almost collapsed. Her mum, Nana Hedges, was visiting to help with the new arrival and she called the doctor who mistakenly diagnosed a post-natal hernia and treated accordingly – but the pain persisted and worsened over the coming days and weeks, often leaving mum completely bed-ridden.

Dad took on a lot of the burden of looking after his baby daughter as well as Eira and myself but, when mum was admitted to hospital for subsequent surgery around the beginning of October I went to stay with some friends and Ruth was handed over to a lady connected to the corps for a few weeks while mum recovered from her major surgery. To her dismay, when Ruth came back home to her she did not recognize her mummy at all and Ruth cried constantly for a while – what a trauma that must have been and, probably, that episode was the worst disruption to our family there ever was.

As for me, I loved my new little sister immensely and have some very special memories of those early days in her life. Family is so precious and I'm eternally grateful that I was always encouraged to nurture love and respect for mine, both immediate and more distant, in my young life.

I mentioned the Over 60s club earlier and I have some very vivid memories of that group of jolly (and not so jolly!) Yorkshire-folk from the times I spent with them during school holidays. The Over-60s Club Secretary was a dour Yorkshireman called John Willie Dyson. He signed my autograph book with a postage stamp and the inscription 'Bah gum, it's stuck! It's stuck, bah gum!'

Every week the club was preceded by a Luncheon Club and, when on those breaks from school, it was one of the highlights for me to go in the car with my dad to Staincliffe Hospital (again!) and help collect the prepared meals in large metal pots and trays that we would then deliver to the 'hut' to be served to the pensioners. One particular man who attended the club was known to me as Mr Waring, but to many others he was nicknamed 'Old Fish'n'Chips'. For, whatever meal was served up to him, he would complain that it was no good and he would loudly declaim that he wasn't coming again, he'd rather just go and have fish and chips! He still turned up each week, though, so I guess it couldn't have been that bad really!

Another of his quirks was that he claimed not to like rice or semolina puddings and, as these were often part of the menu, he would ask the kitchen for any leftover gravy and pour it over his dessert 'to improve the flavour'. While waiting for his food he would 'entertain' Eira and myself by lighting matches and putting them in his open mouth…a somewhat surprisingly impressive feat to a 7 year old boy, it seems! So much for Mr Waring, old fish'n'chips! So much for Health & Safety!

Amazingly enough, my dad had the luxury of a break from building work during our two years in Heckmondwike. The hall didn't fall down and the hut remained sturdy…there's been a new quarters for the corps since and the hut is, alas, now gone and 'Wembley Stadium' built on – but between 1970 and 1972 it was 'all quiet on the building front! Although I said 'alas' I should say that I only mean that from my own, selfish, childhood point of view – the fact is that the SA has expanded its work in the community enormously through that new building work and making good use of the land they owned!

Dad and I used to walk through the town on a Saturday morning to go and watch the Huddersfield Town apprentices play their home matches at Speck's Lane. Dad was an excellent talent-spotter and could easily point out which player s were going to 'make it' in the game through watching these youngsters. As I may have intimated earlier I was football mad by this time and all my pocket money went on football cards (I'd usually throw the enclosed bubble gum away, only wanting the precious cards) and I was developing an almost encyclopaedic knowledge of 1970s football that I retain to this day. One name I remember dad telling me to watch out for from these games was Stewart Barrowclough. He played one Saturday morning for Barnsley as a flying winger. At one point my dad, standing very close to the touchline shouted advice to him, "Put it through the gap!" Instantly, he 'put it through the gap' and the striker 'put it in the net'! AGAINST US!!!

That was typical of dad and football – even the team he supported was not as important as good football – he taught me how to watch as a neutral and enjoy the game, whoever won. Just a few weeks after this event, Stewart Barrowclough signed for Newcastle United and he went on to score 48 goals in a 424 game career. I wonder how many times subsequently he 'put it through the gap'?

HUDDERSFIELD TOWN AFC   official programme
5p

FOOTBALL LEAGUE — DIVISION ONE
LIVERPOOL
Saturday, February 12th, 1972   Kick-off 2.30 p.m.

Every other Saturday we drove to Huddersfield to watch 'The Terriers' play at their old Leeds Road ground. We were in the district for the one season 'The Town' ever reached the old first division and so players like Frank Worthington, Trevor Cherry, Roy Ellam, Dick Krzywicki and Jimmy Lawson became my heroes. I saw Liverpool play for the first time, Ray Clemence making what is to this day the best save I've ever seen to secure a 0-0 draw.

I also saw the 'holy trinity' of Bobby Charlton, Denis Law and George Best play for Manchester United on October 9th, 1971 – my 9th birthday – and my special birthday treat was a seat in the grandstand for this game! What's more – all three of those absolute legends scored in a 3-0 win for Utd. While writing these words, to my astonishment, I managed to find highlights of this very game on YouTube – what a treat to be able to relive that day after so long! Turns out it was the last time all three of them ever scored in the same match – a historic day and rather unique birthday treat! *(The*

photograph above was taken by a friend after the passing of Sir Bobby Charlton)

Of course, Huddersfield was very much the 'little club down the road' in those days to the 'mighty' Leeds United, just a few miles away (although roles have been reversed now and then in the last few years). It was not a great single season the Terriers had in the top flight but, by a long, long way, the highlight was beating Leeds in the local derby. I'd guess that Terriers fans claimed bragging rights on that win for many years to come! Leeds were the League Champions at the time. Dad and I had even tried to get to the championship deciding match v Arsenal at Elland Road the previous April but were turned away when just a few yards from the turnstile once the authorities decided the ground was full…we never tried to get to a Leeds match again…and I never forgave Leeds, which made Huddersfield's victory on that occasion even sweeter!

My playing experiences in football were always at a most basic level…I LOVED playing but lacked either the physique or skills to make any serious impression. Two boys from my school *were* good – and it was my privilege to play in the same team as them in the cubs – my one game for them resulting in a 9 nil victory. I 'should' have scored but my failure to simply lean my head into the ball when about a foot away from the goal line meant Wayne Bruce completed his hat-trick instead. David Southwick was even better – his 5 goals on that occasion gave me a great opportunity to talk to his attractive, blonde sister Lynda, who just happened to be in my class and sat at my table in school! I was growing up!

Chapter Twelve – Life in a Northern Town

To say I did a lot of growing up in Heckmondwike would be a massive understatement – in fact, it might be one of the biggest understatements of all time! When I sang in a Home League meeting 'Now I Belong to Jesus' it was one of the first times I recall singing a song I'd been asked to sing in order to entertain (and/or bless) other people. When they laughed just ever-so-slightly at a 7 or 8 year old trying to sound sincere as I delivered lines like 'Once I was lost in sin's degradation' I didn't notice – I just knew I wanted to sing and enjoy the sensation of people listening to my efforts… When I performed with that little brass quintet and got a clap at the end I began to experience a world that would captivate me for the rest of my life: Jesus wanted to use ME to sing and play for Him – even in my small corner – and He would multiply my efforts to make it something special.

It was at a Central & West Yorkshire Division Home League rally at the world famous Huddersfield Town Hall (for a Divisional Home League Rally) that my brass-playing solo career began. My dad and I stood on that famous stage, so regularly graced by the likes of Black Dyke Mills Band, and we played a little duet – a Mozart excerpt from Tune a Day, Book 2. I was getting to like the feeling of this…and the first stirrings began to start convincing me that a life of music-making was one in which I would find fulfilment and, also, a wonderful avenue of Christian service.

It was whilst in Heckmondwike that I also started piano lessons with a lady who seemed very, very old. If I remember correctly her name was Mrs Mitchell – and she began to train my fingers to find the notes on a piano keyboard, to appreciate music that didn't have its origins in the Salvation Army and learn the basic rudiments of musical theory. I had a long way to go – but I was on the right road. Music began to speak to my mind, my heart…my soul and my spirit and the urge – no, the burning need! – to play a part in making that music started to drive my life, my leisure time and my fledgling service in the Salvation Army!

But, for now, most of my music-making belonged to the singing company. There were two quite recent SA publications that heavily influenced the music we sang and they were 'Sing for Joy' – Joy Webb's purple-fronted collection of songs and spirituals and the second was a compilation of music titled 'Youthful Praise' and housed in a bright 'electric blue' shiny cover! I'm sure we, like many singing companies worked our way through that book and it holds a very special place in my heart, containing such gems as:

Songs in the Heart

Sing of His Wonderful Love

The Lord is Good

So Very Much

I Want to Sing It

How I Love to Sing

The Lord is Good

Spring Season

The Call To Youth

Add to these some good 'oldies' like 'Children Arise', 'The Giver of Good' and 'We Are Soldiers Fighting for the King of Kings' as well as new additions to the singing company repertoire like 'Close By Jesus' by Bill Davidson ("I've just learned the meaning of the word tenacity, I will show vivacity, I'll not let Jesus down") and I was a very happy 'musketeer' in Hecky Singing Company. As well as the boys brass quintet Singing Company programmes featured timbrels (popular 'moves included 'waff', cricket stumps, trombone and 'sea sickness') and a few excellent recitations – one that sticks in my mind was performed by Gilliam Sims and referred to a simple girl who wanted the vicar to pray for her sick cow. When, later, the vicar took ill she, in turn, prayed the same prayer for him:

'You poor old beast, you do look bad

Your poor old mistress looks so sad.

If you live, you live and, if you die you do,

And that will be the end of you!'

Steven, Glen and I spent many happy hours playing together and visiting each other's' homes – sometimes I felt like I'd moved in with Peter and Mary Lister – and, perhaps, the reader will understand quite how happy I was in Heckmondwike.

My teacher at school was Mrs Ingham – she introduced me to writing both stories and poetry, to reading Enid Blyton's 'Famous Five' books and, I think, instilled a lifelong love of learning. I still have a few schoolbooks with things I'd written…an early poem about an alien from Uranus called 'The Ustranoch' comes to mind as does my own particular 'take' on Aladdin in which the inscription on the magic lamp read:

'stuff stink bombs down the spout and you will get a surprise'

In the margin, in red ink, Mrs Ingham wrote:

'so will you if you write this sort of thing again!'

I think I owe a lot to Mrs Ingham!

There were many individual Salvation Army events that I remember from our stay in Heckmondwike. Both the band and songsters went away for weekend campaigns, I was too young to go but I can recall stories told by my dad of the visit to Hull Icehouse Corps and my mum to Camberslang (near Glasgow). That was where mum, when offered a meat sandwich on Saturday night to be made with meat taken from a tiny sliver of beef presented to her as 'the Sunday joint', declined lest she go hungry on Sunday then stayed peckish again when offered a 'slice of porridge' for breakfast 'fresh' from the top drawer of the dresser!

Special weekends at the corps included the visit of the Divisional Commander Joe Evans, who dedicated Ruth during his visit and an enlightening visit from the British Commissioner (now called Territorial Commander) Will Cooper. Commissioner Cooper stayed with us and I loved his 'down to earth' attitude – he told us how he had recently visited SP&S to buy a new cap and, upon being told that the white and silver braid for a Commissioner's cap was going to be £x told them he'd make do with the plain white and much cheaper bandmaster's cap band instead!

The Officers and Local Officers at Heckmondwike SA with the Brirish Commissioner and Mrs Will Cooper. L to R CSM Arthur Haigh, CT David Thompson, S/coy Ldr Linda Thompson, Major Jean Harry, SL Ron Cost, Major Ken Harry, Comm & Mrs Cooper, CS Arnold Walker

As always, before a visit from a high ranking officer my dad, as the CO, had to contact THQ with information about what pieces the band and songsters had prepared for the weekend. Commissioner Cooper had replied asking, in not so many words, if he was coming for a funeral and could the musical leaders possibly offer something a bit more 'lively'? That was how I learned to love Bram Coles's classic 'Why Hang Your Harp on the Willow?' for that was what the songsters eventually sang!

Apart from mum's illness Heckmondwike also had its share of sadnesses - some awful events that led to me 'growing up' in ways I hadn't previously had to: firstly, a young lady athlete I had admired since winning a silver medal at the 1968 Olympic Games died after a battle with cancer. Lillian Board had seemed so young, so full of life, so untouchable – yet here she was teaching me how life isn't always fair. In the corps the songster leader's wife died a tragic and terrible death due to the ravages of cancer. I remember the effect Mrs Cost's illness had on my father as he tried to prepare her husband and family for her impending passing. He would return home from visiting her, his face drawn, and share with my mum over the family dining table his obvious distress – he hadn't meant to, of course, but the stresses a young Salvation Army officer had to deal with sometimes just cannot be hidden. Likewise the tragedy when a young couple in the corps suffered a tragic cot death, long before most of the world knew such occurrences happened. The little girl had been in our front room at the quarters just a short time before and I had sat looking at this beautiful little girl, not much younger than my own little sister…and then she was gone…I therefore became aware of the reality of death in Heckmondwike – and the consequences of serious illness. I began to pray that God would keep us from such terrible things.

The things we had to deal with were, as you'd expect, mere trivialities in comparison. One day. While paying football in 'Wembley Stadium' with my friend Colin Greenwood I smashed a window in the SA hall…it might as well have been a tragedy for me at the time though! Then Ruth, my lovely little sister toppled over while in her baby-walker (above) and smashed her face into the floor resulting in much blood and tears – not nice at all but still better than I'd seen others go through…

…And, another day, Steven and I were playing cricket outside the old hut using a gnarled old elderberry tree as our cricket stumps. I hit the ball high over extra cover and the ball became lodged on the hut roof. The area between the hut and the perimeter wall was something of a wilderness – full of weeds, overgrown shrubs and small trees – but we ventured forth in search of the lost ball nevertheless. It was a hot day, which I remember clearly, and Steven – being considerably more agile than me – shinned up a drainpipe and climbed onto the roof of the hut. He hadn't been up there long before he spotted the errant ball and, making his way across to it he muttered an exclamation as his foot slipped.

The next thing I remember was a sharp bang on the head and I put my hand up to the source of the pain. With Steven now descended from the roof (complete with ball) we made our way round to the front of the hut again before he looked up and I could tell from the semi-scream he made that something was wrong. I took my hand away from my head and immediately realized the problem – my hand was absolutely covered in blood and, of course, I started to cry! Steven shouted so loud my parents heard in the flat and, within minutes, I was on my way to the hospital to have stitches inserted in a wound caused by Steven's dislodging of a house brick from the roof of the hut. Ouch! Oh, that hut! I once found a gun underneath it…did I mention that?

When farewell orders came to my parents in April 1972 followed swiftly by marching orders informing us that our new home was to be 374 miles away – almost at the tip of Cornwall – it was the only time I ever cried at the prospect of having to move.

On the day of our Farewell Meeting I'm told that Steven, Glen and I sat at the back of the hall long after the meeting finished, steadfastly refusing to move in protest. It was, of course, to no avail – the SA had spoken and mum and dad, being obedient officers, obeyed the call. We were on our way to Camborne and, in retrospect, I was to have no reason to regret that at all.

Chapter Thirteen – Heckmondwike Appendices

These are two additional pieces of writing that were inspired by the time I lived in Heckmondwike. The first is an item I wrote for the corps when the old hut was finally demolished in Spring 2011. In 2012 I returned to the Corps to lead Songster Weekend, conducting a rehearsal and concert with massed Songster Brigades on the Saturday afternoon and evening then leading the meetings on Sunday along with my mum. Please excuse some story repetitions already mentioned in this book's main narrative but this was a piece written 'from the heart' in reference to a real-time event.

The 2nd is a published poem 'Life in a Northern Town' from my first collection of poems 'Cortina Biriani' (1995).

Bloomin' Oomah! They're Knocking the 'ut Down!

I moved to the exquisitely named West Riding town of Heckmondwike in 1970. Just thinking back to our first drive up a muddy side road (Barracks Street) is enough to start the memories flowing and transporting me back to a bygone era like Sam Tyler in a Yorkshire version of 'Life On Mars'. There was a park opposite, a sweet shop on the corner and a strange little garage that stretched from the main road to the Army gates. The garage sold and repaired those funny little pale blue invalidity cars that dad and I used to joke that Huddersfield Town let in free - but if you drove one to Leeds Utd. they expected you to play!

To place it in time we moved to 'Ecky a fortnight or so after The Beatles broke up - I can vividly picture 'early Heckmondwike' copies of dad's Daily Mirror with photos of John, George and Ringo and various mooted Paul replacements as the world mourned the Fab Four. Just a few weeks later the greatest football team yet to grace this planet won the World Cup in Mexico: Pele, Jairzinho, Gerson, Tostao, Carlos Alberto and Rivelino are names forever ingrained into my mind. They barely scraped past a determined England (Gordon Banks and all!) but demolished Italy in the final and that performance is not only given its legendary status by what my 7 year old mind can recall but by all the experts from all around the football world too.

We lived in the flat above the Army Hall - Barrack House was a name grander than it probably deserved but it was a fine home for us for the next two years; indeed the first house for my baby sister Ruth who was born just three months later. I recall mum setting fire to the chip pan, I remember shaking the ketchup bottle so hard the lid came off and painted the kitchen ceiling red - and I can recall the biggest back garden a 7 year old boy could have ever wished for!

In the beginning we had a veranda! I didn't even know what one was before! It was where mum had her washing line and where I played '3 and in' with my younger (not youngEST) sister, Eira. I wasn't that bad a goalie so it took her a good, long time to get her three goals. MY 'outfield' time was a) considerably shorter and b) eternally frustrating - for my sister had usually got bored by then! She would disappear to the other end of the veranda and come back with a bright orange Spacehopper:

"I'm so rubbish in goal this is as good as me!" she would declaim before retiring indoors to play with her Cindy dolls and leaving me to shoot against the inflatable, immobile, orange blob of plastic. (It was still better than Gary Sprake, though!)

As time passed it also became clear that, IF Mr S Hopper, esq. DID manage to make a save he couldn't catch! The ball would rebound in a random direction, usually completely OFF the veranda and down into the Car Park. If I wanted to carry on playing I had a long walk downstairs to fetch my ball!

I wrote earlier that we lived in the flat above the main Salvation Army Hall and so there was also the afore-mentioned car park beside the hall - and I soon moved my football epics from the veranda downstairs to the muddy wasteland that doubled as said car park or my personal football pitch (dependant, of course, on time and day of the week) - after all - as I said this WAS my back garden!

So I booted my ball endlessly against a massive concrete wall (behind which was one of many carpet factories then situated within the boundaries of the mile-square town). To the other side of the car park/personal Wembley...was a large wooden hut!

I probably have more memories of that hut than I do the main hall! It was where we had Sunday School twice every Sabbath for a start. I had two very good friends back then - Steven, Glen and I were affectionately nicknamed 'The Three Musketeers' by Linda, our Singing Company Leader (Junior Church Choir) and I dread to think what traumas we put our Sunday School teachers through...

I DO recall a Summer Holiday Club in the hut and lots of new 'non-Army' children who attended along with us regulars. While on one side of the hut was the car park the other side was a mini-jungle of weeds, small trees and stinging nettles. I recall a girl called Jane (one of the 'new' girls at the club) who reckoned she was fitter than 'The Three Musketeers' and she invited us to chase her around the whole compound, starting at the back of the hut ' jungle-side' and ending up (I remember...for some reason...ahem!) near the concrete steps up to our flat. Steven caught her first, followed by me and I waited impatiently while he claimed his promised prize - A KISS of all things! - and I just got round to getting mine before our impromptu adventure was ended by a puffing Steven's dad, Peter, coming round the corner of the hall and dragging us all back to the official Holiday Club activities. (I reckon our activities were more fun, though!)

Peter was one of three people from Heckmondwike I remember particularly fondly and who each had a profound effect on my young life. I stayed at the Lister home many times during those two years and Peter's friendship continued with our family for many years after our move away - long after I'd lost all contact with Steven and right up to Peter's tragically early death through cancer (followed, so soon by Mary, his wife, too). I have also remained friends with the choir leader, Linda. The third was a man we called (behind his back) The Giant! George Brooke, the corps Bandmaster must have been close to seven feet tall...but if he was a giant he was, indeed, a gentle and patient one. It was he who taught us musketeers to play the cornet and, along with two other young brothers, Mark and Ian Walker, we formed a brass quintet with special pieces composed by George himself - one unforgettably arranged around the Sunday School chorus 'A Woman Came to Fill Her Water Pot'. We used to call it 'FillaWottaPot' and the audiences always laughed when little Ian Walker (who despite being the smallest of the five of us had the largest instrument - a baritone) descended the scale to a very low note on the words 'Down at the bottom of the well'! I guess we were like sons to George who seemed to all intents to be a confirmed bachelor - well, if we were it turned out to be good practice for, to all our surprise, he later married and spawned boy triplets! Bless him!

By the door of the hut was a large elderberry tree. I used to love picking the deliciously sweet, tiny black berries when they miraculously appeared each year. Because someone told me they were used to make elderberry wine I used to pretend the berries made me drunk - always a show-off looking for an opportunity to entertain my pals even back then! For the summer holiday, though, that tree was my cricket stumps, that patch of land was Lords and a school-friend Colin Greenwood and I played endless test matches there, every bit as serious as the real ones dad watched Boycott and Illingworth play upstairs in the flat on our rented black and white telly! Hitting the ball into the car park was good for running 3 or 4, out of the gates into Barracks Street you might get straight-driven 5 but a leg-side slog through the elder leaves into the big Public Car Park was a precious six!

It strikes me now as strange that playing on church property, as we were, I should recall that Public Car Park as a sort of 'Holy Ground'...but so it became one day when Harold Wilson came and stood on a soap box husting in that very Car Park - and we stood on the steps of the hut entrance and saw this little man in his beige raincoat hold the attention of his Socialist supporters for an hour or so - occasionally puffing on his pipe - and my dad wondered if he held the corps-folk as rapt during his Sunday sermons?

It seems to me now that everything that happened during the week at the 'Army' happened in the 'hut'. There was 'Knitters Fellowship' of all things (which occupied the ladies while the men were in Band Practice - despite there being some ladies in the band...so it wasn't a sexist thing by any means!), Over-Sixties Club and Home League Meetings also took place in the hut and I have some vivid memories of the former in particular!

Over-Sixties was always preceded by Luncheon Club and there was nothing we children liked doing more during the school holidays than going with dad in the car to pick up the big aluminium trays and pots from Staincliffe Hospital in nearby Dewsbury. It must have been the hospital canteens that prepared the food for the Luncheon Club and it was always rather exciting (were we really THAT sad?) to get them into the hut and open the lids to see if dessert that week was rice pudding or semolina!

One old man I will never forget! He was known to us all as 'Old Fish and Chips' but his real name was Mr Waring. He was tall, bald and smelt of cigarettes. He would entertain my sister and I by doing silly conjuring tricks and by lighting matches and putting them in his mouth. We thought he was wonderful...the rest of the club and its leaders , however, did not agree. Whatever food was served up, every week without fail, he would complain, call the food disgusting and declare that he didn't know why he came and he'd "Rather have fish and chips!" - Hence his nickname! He also claimed to detest the desserts (whether rice or semolina it seems) and went, without fail, to round up any leftover gravy from the main course with which to smother his otherwise unpalatable bowlful! My sister and I watched him in near disbelief eating every morsel of his rice pudding and gravy! And, despite his protestations about the awfulness of the food he was always back the next week for more - again, without fail!

One particular memory of the hut concerned the day I went to fetch my ball when it went underneath...and found a gun! This was close to our leaving Hecky (I remember because I was in my 2nd year at Millbridge Upper in Liversedge - Mrs Ingham's class). I was too scared to even tell my mum and dad for a couple of days but that didn't stop me going back down to the hut after dark with a torch to check that the gun (which was wrapped carefully in a dark red cloth) was still there! Eventually I told my dad and he came with me to see - only to inform me it was merely an air pistol and the 'bullets' were little pellets. Far from making the front page of the local paper or helping the police solve a macabre murder dad found an old dart board and showed me how he had learned in his REME National Service to take aim and 'fire'. Eventually we bought some compatible 'darts' and made less damage to the dartboard - and we kept my 'lethal weapon' for very many years!

But, probably, the most lingering memory of the hut was the one that sent me to hospital! On this occasion the elderberry test match opponent was Steven and one shot of mine looked like it was going to end the match prematurely. It looped upwards and 'off-side' up onto the hut's sloping roof and, we presumed, into the 'jungle'. We searched for some time to no avail when Steven decided that the ball must have somehow lodged on the hut's roof!

"You stay here and I'll climb up and have a look," he instructed me - so I stood guard (as though climbing on the hut roof was a cardinal, or at least arrestable, sin!)

No sooner had I heard him shout, "Found it!" than something hit my head. With my hand still on the offended portion of head Steven and I made to return to our game. It's funny how I remember the pain but know for a fact I wasn't crying...until Steven said, "Look at your hand!" and I did!

He had inadvertently dislodged an old house brick from the hut roof and it was that that had struck my head. When I looked at my hand it was covered in blood - and THAT was the cue for the tears and screaming to start! This alerted my parents (as did Steven - I told you he was the fastest runner!) shooting off to the flat, and within minutes we were speeding towards the hospital for the measly TWO stitches they undoubtedly saved my young life with!! Oh, the trauma!

****

And the hut is now to be demolished, they tell me - later this month no less. The side of my Wembley, the Elderberry Lords Pavilion, the source of my stitches and where I found the gun...where Mr Waring lit his matches and ate rice pudding and gravy, where the knitters made garments uncountable...and it was also the hut where I, undoubtedly, knelt in prayer as a young lad at the start of a Christian journey that still continues today. So, I think of the others who sang with me over 40 *(edit – now 50)* years ago in that Singing Company: Jennifer, Jeanette, Gillian (whose recitation about a cow I can still recite today!), Steven, Mark, Ian etc. (Glen and Sarah are still Facebook friends). Do they all remember kneeling in the hut too? I hope so...and I pray their thoughts turn in its direction sometimes no matter what life has dealt them in the intervening years. God Bless them all!

They can take away the hut...but no-one can destroy my precious memories. I'm glad I've put them on paper to share...they've probably had enough of being locked up in my brick-damaged head all these years!

Life in a Northern Town *(from 'Cortina Biriani' 2005)*

Walking to school was never a drag

With Lochead, Greenwood and Eira

And school itself was never so bad,

Unless you sat next to Myra!

For Myra was smelly (it wasn't her fault)...

I sat next to Lynda – I wasn't a dolt!

Walking to school we passed by a mill

And a garage that kept changing hands.

We smiled at the Indian with ginger hair

And picked up the stray rubber bands

That were left by the postman – and went on to school.

I learned with Miss Ingham – I wasn't a fool.

On the corner of Barracks Street there was a shop

Which we passed on our way to the school

And there we bought bubble gum and football cards

And lollies so we could stay cool.

Through a small basement window we shouted at 'Nelly'

So she sprayed us with hair lacquer – ever so smelly!

I played in the yard on my own and with pals,

Bursting my 'Bobby Moore' ball.

For goalie I used a big, orange spacehopper

As I tried to hit the far wall.

While playing with Steven, he dislodged a brick

Which hit my poor head – to the hospital, quick!

Steven and me, we just couldn't be parted

And, when I had to leave, we were near broken-hearted.

With Glen, Mark and Ian we'd started a band

And we practiced for hours...wasn't it grand?

"A woman came to fillowotopot,

Down at the bottom of the well!"

And what about Tuesdays? Dad's luncheon club?

We'd drive to pick up the food

And John Willie Dyson and 'old Fish 'n chips

Would complain, "bah gum, it's no good'!"

Ha! Old Mr Waring ate rice pud with gravy...

(I wonder if Leeds ever signed up young Davy?)

It's long ago now but I haven't forgotten

My friends and the places I liked.

The walks to the market, the pool (and the barber!)

In greyish old Heck-a-mondwike.

If I go back there now, it'll still be the same

But life just goes on – aint that a shame?

<u>Chapter Fourteen – North to South</u>...and <u>Nearly to Land's</u> End

After three homes in three years in Yorkshire the Harrys were 'on the move' again – and, this time, it was all the way down to Cornwall. I'd never been to Cornwall although, of course, I was aware of its existence and I knew that many people went there for holidays. It seemed a very long way and I recall that we broke our (nearly 400 mile) journey by stopping with family overnight part way through the trek south and west.

Something very few people ever grasp is that the distance from London to Land's End is more than 25 miles further than from London to Newcastle...and, in 1972 and for many years after that, the roads to the South West were considerably less manageable than the A1. The old A30 was a single carriageway road right through Devon, across the top of Dartmoor and Bodmin Moor, and then on through the length of Cornwall. In summer thousands of holiday-makers crammed the roads creating a seemingly perpetual traffic jam. London to Camborne could easily be an eight hour journey – enough time to comfortably drive from London to Dundee!

But...was it worth it? Oh yes! For, in the next two years I fell in love with the county and, in so many ways, my life changed forever and for the better! For a start, the old tin-mining town of Camborne was, literally, surrounded by beaches! I've always loved the seaside but we'd never been privileged to live within easy travelling distance of it. We holidayed each summer at one of the Salvation Army's hotels, either in Broadstairs, Margate or Bournemouth and my maternal grandparents lived in St Leonard's-on-Sea near Hastings but this was the first time we had been able to jump in the car and be on a beach within half an hour. And not just ONE beach? From Camborne we could be in Portreath, Gwithian, St Agnes, Newquay, Perranporth, Hayle, Porthtowan, St Ives or Penzance (to name just a few) within just a short drive – and I'm glad to say we made the most of those opportunities over the next couple of years. I developed a love for all these places and I have returned to this part of Cornwall, especially Portreath, most years for my own family holidays over the past few decades.

If the location itself wasn't good enough to be near unbelievable, the officer's quarters in Camborne was by far the best accommodation we had ever lived in. From the old, terraced houses of Newport and Bargoed to the simple flat above the hall at Heckmondwike we were transported to a beautiful, large, detached bungalow at the end of a private close with a front lawn the size of a bowling green, a back garden the size of half a football pitch – and with endless cow fields behind that and a disused stone quarry to one side. We only had two sets of direct neighbours: The Jeffreys, whose father ran the Funeral Director business near the SA Hall, and another couple that we rarely met but we were more aware of their 2 Old English Sheepdogs. Further down the close lived a reclusive former Naval Commander, Mr Rodgers who, over time, we managed to befriend.

The quarry made a wonderful adventure playground. We called it 'The Burrows' and we spent more time in The Burrows than we did our own gardens. It was full of rocks that contained iron pyrites (fool's gold) and beautiful crystal quartz. Eira, in particular, loved the quartz and collected boxes full of it. (When we left Camborne she was told to throw it all away – only later did we see shops opening selling lesser examples than her collection for £25 or more a piece!)

Eira and I enrolled at Roskear County Primary School just a short walk down the hill and along Dolcoath Road. The Salvation Army Hall was one of the very few 'Fortresses', just set back from the main shopping street in the town and was a large, rambling building with a platform and gallery and a massive upstairs area known as the 'Glory Shop'.

Camborne Corps was a vibrant place with a good band, large songsters and a thriving YP Corps. Again, there was no YP Band but a very good singing company with many other children was again a thrill to join in with. I grew to love that corps in a way I have never loved any other and it almost broke my heart when it closed in 2015…but more of that later.

Better, for now, to concentrate on what was – and the mark that Camborne Salvation Army Corps made on a young man…

To write about Camborne corps I simply have to concentrate on the lovely, genuine people who made up the corps – and I can do no better than to start with a man who remained a good friend right up until his Promotion to Glory a few years ago – Bandmaster Ken Norton.

Of all the great jobs in the world to have Ken owned a fish and chip shop! That gave him an instant, infinite credit in this nine year old boy's book – wow! And the shop literally backed onto the front of the SA hall! Ken used to come to band practice straight from work and the wonderful scent of freshly gutted cod was forever on his hands (That's not to say it was a 'fishy' smell for that would mean stale fish – this was a scent fresh as a trawlerman's net). Ken had the broadest West-Country burr you could ever imagine and I rarely recall him without a smile on his face. He welcomed me into the senior band even at my tender age of nine and having never played in a 'proper' band at all before. I played cornet alongside he and the Songster Leader Roger Wills but, sadly, Roger left the band part-way through our time in Camborne and, when Ken went into hospital for a hernia operation, I was left as the only cornet player in the band for a few months. I KNOW that this was a period of time when my playing improved dramatically (through necessity, I think!) and it was a relief when another excellent cornettist, Brian Driver, transferred to the corps from Derbyshire and his tone and finesse inspired me to practice even harder.

Two of Ken's favourite pieces were the hymn tune arrangements St Agnes and St Ethelwald and these we played very often, as we also did Eric Ball's transcription of 'The Pilgrim's Prayer'. Ken was not a 'stand out front and wave' bandmaster – he always led the band from his cornet seat – but that didn't seem to harm the ensemble and he could listen while playing and always seemed to know where any problems in the ensemble lay. He was an astute musician who had two of his compositions published in The Musical Salvationist (a quarterly publication of music for SA Songster Brigades), one of which made it into Gems 7 – a compilation of the most popular songs over a decade or so.

But it was a more auspicious and difficult band piece that I remember playing with Camborne Band the most memorably. Ken's father, himself a former BM at the corps in years gone by, was still alive when we went to Camborne, although he was very old and very poorly. As he neared the end of his earthly life his one desire was to hear just once more Arthur Gullidge's beautiful band selection 'Divine Communion'. This was too difficult a piece for the band to usually manage and was scored for General Series – a larger ensemble than the band could boast – but I can recall standing in the street outside his bedroom and the dozen or so of us who were there played that beautiful and memorable piece. As the music filled the air it seemed that the angels joined in – a true 'Divine Communion indeed. It could have been the best band in the world playing that morning and God felt so close to us all as we prayed in music together,

'Sweet will of God, still fold me closer,

Til I am wholly lost in Thee'

The band regularly played concerts – I can recall going to several churches out in some of the quaintly named tiny Cornish villages such as Praze-an-Beeble and Zelah and we had a yearly engagement at a holiday camp in St Ives that we used to look forward to.

Ken most certainly took me 'under his wing' and was a constant encourager to a lad learning to find his feet both as a young musician and, much more importantly, as a young Christian. Later in life, when I returned to Camborne corps every summer for many years with my children he would always have instruments ready for us and extra seats for us to help swell the band-which was often down to 4 or 5 members by then. The last time we met was during our regular fortnight's camping holiday in Portreath and the band actually scheduled a rehearsal – their first one for many years – because Morgan, Lewis and I had promised to attend. I know it was a thrill for the humble bandsmen (and bandswoman) to play through a whole succession of Unity Series marches and selections for about an hour and I treasure that memory so preciously. My eldest son, Morgan wanted to be photographed with Ken, who he obviously recognized as one of my 'faith heroes' and I treasure that photograph too – for before our next holiday Ken had gone to be with the Lord he had loved and served for so many years. *(Below, Ken and my eldest son Morgan)*

Ken's wife, Kath, also worked with him in the chip shop and it was many years later that my parents admitted the little trick she used to help her commanding officers stretch their salary a little. If mum went into the shop to buy a meal for us she would pay Kath with a pound note and, when she checked her change she would often find it consisted of 2 x 50p coins. Every little helps!

Those 50p coins came in handy! I continued my piano lessons in Camborne with a most 'interesting teacher'. Harry Apps was completely blind and lived, with his wife, in a large house just down the hill from us in Dolcoath Close. Mr. Apps had just a small number of books that he could teach from as he needed to own them in braille and he would sit with these enormous volumes on his lap behind me and follow the melodies through. There was 'Scenes at a Farm' by Walter Carroll and, when that had been exhausted we moved onto 'Tunes From Nature'…by Walter Carroll and then, just for a change, 'Buried in a Pig-Sty up to my Flipping Neck' by Walter Flapjack with seven zeds and a silent P! If my fingers were as bored stiff as the rest of me no wonder they kept playing wrong notes!

Even worse, each piece had a little poem that went with it…but Mr. Apps thought they were lyrics. Now, even the most cursory glance would tell anyone with half a brain cell that these poems did not fit the tunes at all…but Mr. Apps never let that stop him and, as I concentrated on making 'Oops, I Trod in a Cowpat last Thursday Morning' sound as musical as I could (surprisingly there wasn't a piece called 'Look What I Can Do With a Sow's Ear!') Mr. Apps would sing along in his cracked baritone. It was probably a very good job he couldn't see my face!

Then, one day while we were 'Out in a Boat' it all got too much for him. He began by telling me my errors were making him seasick and, after a few more wrong notes had him tipped out of the boat and splashing around in the water he stopped the lesson and sent me home. Before I got there he had rung my father with the news that I was on my way, that he had returned this week's 50p and that I wasn't to go back ever again! In his expert opinion he told my disappointed father that he was wasting his money – I would NEVER MAKE A MUSICIAN!!

It so happens that my younger sister, Eira, had started piano lessons by then as well but, somehow, she had escaped the attentions of Professor Apps – she was learning with a younger lady who lived in one of the terraced streets near the army hall and whose name, if I recall correctly, was Serena Bartle (?). So she agreed to take me on as well and I got my second chance to learn. She put me straight onto a book called 'Album for the Young' by Schumann and, within a few weeks I was playing 'A Little Chorale', 'Siciliano' and attempting 'The Wild Horseman' on my own and without being told to because it was the last one in the book, looked hard and because I was now enjoying playing! Thank you Serena!

About a decade later, when mum and dad went back down to Cornwall for a holiday, dad could not resist going to see Mr. Apps…he still lived in the big old house. Oh yes, he remembered me and his pronouncement of my incapability. Dad proudly let him now that I had just graduated from Music College with a top BA honours degree. I BET THAT FELT GOOD!

Chapter Fifteen – Camborne – The Testimony Corps

What I remember most about Camborne Corps will always be the way that the dear comrades of that corps made use of what we in The Salvation Army call the 'testimony period'. This is a section of a meeting, morning or evening, where the CO chooses a few choruses and, between them, the local corps folk are free to speak about their recent experiences as a Christian and how the Lord has helped them to share the Gospel or their faith with others. Sadly, there are many officers today who undervalue this part of worship (often, it seems, the ones who prefer the sound of their own voices!) but my parents were keen to allow such expressions of spontaneity into their meetings and I, as a young, growing Christian lad, soaked up the testimony periods at Camborne with a wide-eyed hunger.

To tell of my experiences it is best to tell of the testimonies themselves – for they are forever etched into my memory like beacons of fire, marking my life forever. Our YPSM (Young People's Sergeant-Major, the lady 'in charge' of the Sunday School) was Holly Jose. Her husband, Bill, was the Corps Sergeant-Major. Holly's mother, Mrs. George was absolutely stone deaf but she was ever present in the meetings and sat near the back on the left as you looked from the platform, beside a window and a radiator. The radiator was not always just for warmth, though – Mrs. George had long realized that she could feel vibrations through the radiator whenever the band played and she would often testify thanking the band for their contribution to the meetings and the blessings she received through their playing – just by feeling and interpreting these vibrations. You just KNEW she meant it – God really was blessing her in this way and I was amazed that our wonderful God could do such a thing!

Mrs. George and Holly Jose came from a family called Smith that had had an association with Camborne Corps right from its earliest days. I always thought (my memory told me it was from my father's words) that there was a connection with the early Salvation Army days of the famous evangelist and singer Gypsy Smith but I have recently found out this may not be so and the two families may well have no actual link. There were certainly other members of the Smith family involved in the SA, though and remained so as long as the corps survived.

Tragically, part of the way through our time in Camborne, Mrs. George was fatally injured on a pedestrian crossing outside Woolworths in the High Street and, for the first time I can ever remember, I was able to experience a real, old-fashioned Salvation Army funeral. It was anything but a sad occasion with joyful songs, clapping and tambourines, a march from the band and more. The band even marched right into the cemetery and up to the grave – in single file by that point – still playing and waving the flag as Mrs. George was literally waved onto the Hallelujah Strand to the angels' 'welcome home'. I still often think of that occasion when I attend sombre, black and tearful funerals – and, when my time comes (God-willing a long time from now!) I know which version I would prefer!

Just in front of Mrs. George sat Mrs. Rochelle. Mrs. Rochelle was a lady who did not wear Salvation Army uniform but always wore a very fetching red and white hat, She came to the meetings with another lady, a tiny, uniformed soldier called Suzie Smith. We were in Camborne when Sunderland beat Leeds Utd.in the FA Cup Final and their manager Bob Stokoe ran onto the hallowed, Wembley turf at the end of the game wearing his own red and white hat – I always thought he would have loved to have had Mrs. Rochelle's hat - already in his club's colours! But I digress…Mrs. Rochelle was almost always the first on her feet in the testimony period – especially if there was even a hint of silence before anyone else rose to speak. Then she would say,

"I know you're all tired of my voice but, if you don't want to hear me, get to your feet first!"

Then she would read her latest poem. She was clearly often inspired to write little poems at home during the week and would then bring them with her on Sundays to share with the rest of us. How I wish someone had had the foresight to collect them for her and publish them in a little booklet for posterity but, alas, they are gone now forever. Then, there was old Mr. Mitchell on the other side of the hall. He would also regularly testify in his deep, gruff and croaky voice – and he would end each time by breaking into his favourite chorus,

"He's the Christ of the human road

And He offers to carry your load,

He is walking your way

144

Every night, every day,

This Christ of the human road.

He is human and, yet, so Divine

And He knows your heart's sorrow and mine.

In all kinds of need

He's a true friend indeed,

This Christ of the human road."

Of course, the moment he began speaking Bandmaster Ken Norton would very subtlely move over to the organ and, as the gruff-voiced old man started to sing, he would be ready with the accompaniment so that the rest of the congregation could join in.

Having had one testimony from the left and one from the right it seemed only fitting that the next should come from the middle bank of seats – and so it was as a very old, frail lady would stand and tell us some amazing stories of how her dear Lord was able to use her in her limited capacity to help, encourage and bless others that she met – and she would always tell us how she wished she could still do more for God. Mrs. Calloway was another lovely lady and I often went to speak to her after the meetings. She was always ready to give her testimony in the meeting because she just couldn't 'hold in' how good God was to her and how much she loved Jesus. At the end of Mrs. Calloway's testimony she always used to say the same words:

"You can TAKE THE WORLD – but GIVE ME JESUS! For….."

And, again, Ken would swell a chord on the organ for her to lead us all in another chorus of,

"He's all I need, He's all I need. Jesus is all I need."

Well over twenty years later I went to an old people's home with Portsmouth Citadel Songsters to do a programme for Harvest and I was asked to perform the function of auctioneer for the selling of the donated harvest produce. So, I sold the carrots, apples and boxes of breakfast cereal, bread, jam and pumpkins…with my eye firmly on a beautiful, home-made Cornish pasty that sat on a plate amongst the other produce.

Having mentioned that I had lived in Camborne during my 'sales-talk' a little old lady resident in the home spoke to me afterwards to tell me that she was also from that Salvation Army corps. Not only that but she was a retired Salvation Army Officer! She eventually told me that, although she had left home long before the time we lived there, her mother would have still attended at that time. When she told me her mother was Mrs. Calloway I immediately shared with her the thoughts I have just outlined above and we sat together, tears flowing in that care home and then we sang together that same old chorus. It meant a lot to her that day that her mother's testimonies had so inspired and helped a 9 year old lad on his own Christian journey – and there I was so many years later still travelling life's road with the same Jesus I had so often heard Mrs. Calloway sing about, her arms outstretched and raised to Heaven as she sang. Lovely and amazing memories.

In the same 'row' as Mrs. Calloway sat some other elderly ladies – one of whom was Mrs. Woodcock. Her son, Lloyd Woodcock, was my headmaster at Roskear School (although I didn't know that at the time!). Another of the ladies was called Mrs. Billings. She was completely blind and I remember that several of these ladies later came with us on a Corps Over-Sixties holiday to Llandrindod Wells in central Wales. I occasionally found myself privileged to sit next to Mrs. Billings on the coach, describing the beautiful scenery as we drove through the hills and valleys beside the reservoirs in the Elan Valley. On our very last Sunday in the corps she spoke to my dad, thanking him for his ministry – and happened to let him know that his Welsh accent had caused her a 'little' problem: whenever dad had said 'God' in the past two years during meetings she had thought he'd been saying 'guard' and had only twigged his intended meaning on that very last day! Not a lot of what dad had said must have made much sense to dear old Mrs. Billings, I guess but, in her heart I know she must have loved Jesus and she was there, every week, for all the right reasons.

There were others who testified at Camborne, of course. I remember the Corps Treasurer Ernie Hazleton who would also announce it was a 'Glory, Hallelujah' week if the weekly cartridge/offerings amounted to more than twenty pounds. Ernie, a keen gardener, used to bring the most beautiful potted plants every year to be given as gifts on Mother's Day – wonderfully coloured gloxinias, if I recall correctly.

But, last and most definitely not least, I must mention Retired Corps Sergeant-Major Joe Francis. Joe must have been well into his eighties (if not nineties) and was, generally, so infirm that his attendance at meetings was limited to just a few times a year. He still had the very old-fashioned style of SA uniform with navy blue lion-tamer stripes on his tunic and flashy-looking red trimmings – as well proudly wearing his long service medals – it all made him look like a true military war hero!

My sisters and I at the Minnack Theatre – obviously on a Sunday afternoon drive when I had been disinclined to change out of my army uniform.

My Dad used to say that, if Joe Francis got his feet in the meeting, he would put his sermon away – for it was never going to be needed! Joe started by standing where he had been sat but, as he spoke, he made his way around the hall, stopping here and there and speaking, in his loud 'open air voice' about his love of God, about the old days of The Salvation Army and issuing challenges to each succeeding generation about what we were doing today!

Occasionally he would stop and break into an old chorus that we would all join in (if we knew it! – one of his favourites was *"At the end of our journey we shall wear a crown"* – which I soon grew to know despite its age and disuse!) but many of the other corps-folk, whether inspired by this old Spiritual War Hero or shamed by his challenges to us fitter and more able soldiers, would very soon be lining the Mercy Seat in prayer and rededication of their lives to the service of God. THAT is why dad knew he wouldn't need his sermon notes – because, when Joe Francis spoke, the Holy Spirit took over the whole meeting and any man-made plans and preparations became superfluous and completely unnecessary. To this day I continue to be inspired by Joe Francis and his testimonies and, I think, I owe to him a lot of my love for the early history of The Salvation Army.

Joe and his wife were both Promoted to Glory during the two years we were in Camborne, but his influence stays with this then 'Junior Soldier' well over fifty years later – as does the willingness and enthusiasm of the other Camborne 'saints' who testified for their Lord. How I thank God for those testimony periods and the influence these Godly folk had on me then and now.

Mum and dad had a beautiful 'team ministry' throughout their years of officership. Neither of them had the academic qualifications that would be needed today even to become a Salvation Army officer at all but, in those days, the army was more than happy to let God 'qualify the called' rather than just 'call the qualified'- a requirement that seems to be more the case in recent years. They both took an equal part in the ministry so, if dad preached in the morning, mum would do so in the evening. I know it took both a long time to prepare their 'sermon notes' – often both of them hand wrote their talks although dad also used an electric typewriter.

The army has always held a special 'Commitment Sunday' at the beginning of each New Year – one of the first Sundays in January – and the most powerful message I ever witnessed my mum deliver came on one of those at Camborne. She spoke right to the hearts of her congregation and, when she summed up her message by using Will Brand's beautiful song "When from sin's dark hold Thy love had won me" the Holy Spirit again moved strongly in our midst. It was the first time I ever remember extra chairs having to be added to the Mercy Seat as it was already full while more wanted to come and kneel. Every time we reached the chorus I remember the impact of those words, "While Thy presence and Thy power enfold me, I renew my covenant with Thee."

It is mum's exhortation to renew that covenant I STILL hear every January on Commitment Sunday!

Chapter Sixteen – Growing up in (and away from) the Army

As far as being a young lad in the Army at Camborne goes I have already mentioned how I was privileged to be allowed to play with the senior band from the age of 9 – there being no YP Band. This developed my playing no end and I practiced regularly to try to ensure this progress. About two thirds of the way through our stay in Camborne I moved from cornet onto Tenor Horn – BM Ken had noticed the cornet was something of a strain for me – the veins used to stand out on my neck when I blew, apparently – and so I went to sit with the horns in a young section with David Smith and Kenwyn Tonkin.

Dave and Kenwyn, along with the BM's son Nicky, Kenwyn's brother Malcolm and another young man from the band were part of a 'rhythm group'. Such groups had sprung up all over the army during the previous ten years in the wake of 'The Joystrings', the official Salvation Army pop group made up of officers, led by Joy Webb and having achieved chart success with their single 'It's an Open Secret' in the early 1960s. It was Joystrings songs I mostly remember this group playing, especially 'Have Faith in God' and 'All Alone'– although they also featured 'Everybody Sing' – a humorous number from the Army's 'follow-up' group to 'The Joystrings' called 'Good News'.

I also valued the opportunity to take part in a Divisional Musical, performing the Gowans/Larsson musical 'Hosea'. Our Songster Leader Roger Wills played the lead role and his 'real life wife' Cheryl played his 'on-stage wife' too. I was friends with the Harkcom children, whose

151

father, Ray, was the officer at St Ives, through officer's children parties at Christmas and some of them played the parts of children in the production. My mum played a Bus Conductor and my dad played 'Alf'. Me? I didn't have a proper part in the show but formed part of the 'Stage Band' – not the pit orchestra but a small ensemble who dressed in SA Uniform and marched to the Open Air Meeting playing 'Down the Street'. This small role was to play an important part in my long-term musical development at the start of our next adventure when we left Camborne, although none of us knew anything about that at the time!

Roger Wills's mum Winnie was my Singing Company Leader at Camborne and we had a very good and well-taught little junior choir at the corps at that time.

While the boys in the Singing Company wore a traditional SA uniform the attire for the girls was rather more 'adventurous' and definitely 'non-regulation' - as you can see from the photo above. Maroon skirts and boleros over white polo neck jumpers topped with the more conventional Singing Company hat on top. In the winter, instead of a coat, the girls also had beautiful maroon and white crocheted ponchos. It looked great but was far from standard uniform and very daring for its day!

I can't remember everyone by name but I'm the one in short trousers (thanks, mum!) and my best friend at the corps (and Sunbury Music Schools to come) Robbie Smith is two to my right. Eira is two to my left. Ruth, my youngest sister, was only 2 years old but she had her own, specially made, Singing Company uniform and acted as 'mascot'!

I mentioned earlier about being moved onto tenor horn. This had an important part to play in my musical development for, no doubt inspired by my 'promotion' towards the 'better' end of the band, I started to practice my playing far more. Dad bought me the book of Eb solos published by the Army and I remember sitting in my bedroom learning to play the solos 'Swiss Melodies' and 'Shepherd of Israel' (see the earlier chapter on Knottingley) until they were as near to perfect as I could get them…hours and hours and hours of self-critical rehearsal that I simply couldn't imagine 10 year olds today having either the inclination or the patience to submit themselves to – but back then we had only 3 TV channels, no computers or consoles and kids' programming lasted for just an hour or so a day…far less distractions.

But there were SOME OTHER distractions. I was happy at
school in Camborne. My main teacher for two years was a Mrs. Davies.
She was a happy, patient, blonde lady and she seemed to smile a lot –
they were all good qualities for me. I recently found one of our class
photos from 1973:

Not only could I remember a lot of names in this picture but,
when I turned it over I discovered we had all written our names on it.
Mrs. Davies is on the left at the end of the 2nd row and then, working
from L to R that row is Carl Pascoe (known to us all, for the kind of
reason children only know, as 'Jungle Bunny'), Denis Moore, me,
Steven Williams, Wayne Brown, Mark King, Douglas Benetto and
William Rogers. The boy on the back row with striking white-blond hair
was David Innes – he moved to Germany and the smart lad in proper
school uniform in the middle of the back row was, for most of my time
in that school, my best friend - Andrew Polkinghorne.

While collecting for the SA's 'self-denial' appeal one February I was most surprised to knock on Mrs. Davies's door! It was as though I thought teachers didn't have lives of their own but were put in boxes at the end of a school day ready for the next morning! We were probably both just as surprised to see the other! Mrs Davies and I met again many years later when I was touring with the SA Rock Band 'Blood and Fire' and we undertook a week-long mission in Launceston, North Cornwall. Mrs. Davies was working as a supply teacher at the school that we, as a group, were based for much of the week. If I remember correctly, her husband was something like Chief Schools Inspector for Cornwall by then. She was again surprised that I still recognized and remembered her but I always feel that I owe a great debt to the educators who had the patience to deal with a young me!

In my final year at Roskear my teacher was a most formidable spinster called Miss Mutton. She smiled a little less often but, I'm sure, had just as much patience. I passed my 'Eleven Plus' exam to go to Grammar School. I even played for the school football team. My dad only came to watch us once – on the occasion I toe poked a penalty miles over the crossbar! Oops!

But the pitch on which we played that day also carries for me happier memories – for on alternate Saturdays I used to meet up with two of my classmates and go to watch Pool FC play their matches. Pool is a small village next to Camborne and home to what was then the last remaining tin mine in England, South Crofty. Most of the team, including my friend Wayne Brown's dad, who played centre-forward, were miners and we would attend their matches to cheer the side on through thick and thin, victory or defeat. My favourite player (whose name I would have known no more then than today) was a short and slightly rotund midfielder with what was left of his curly, ginger hair surrounding his nearly bald head. How I cheered when he scored a 'blinder' from nearly the half-way line one day in a six-nil victory…and how Wayne, Beverley and I teased the opponent's goalkeeper that day as goal after goal passed him on its way into the net.

Beverley Bertram was, just about, the most tomboy-ish tomboy I ever met: she looked a bit like a boy, acted like a boy and played football like one too! But, because Wayne and I were boys and she was a girl she was happy enough at the time for herself to be referred to as 'our shared girlfriend' – although nothing ever even as vaguely 'girlfriend-ish' as holding hands ever occurred between the three of us!

A fly in that particular ointment for me was…I didn't really WANT her to be my girlfriend – at that I had, for the first time in my young life (but FAR from the last) fallen in what I then took for 'love' with someone else! It's strange how I still remember how intense those feelings were as I admired Linda Houghton from afar. In my daydreams I used to imagine us living as husband and wife in some sort of domestic bliss, despite our tender ages! Of course, she barely knew I existed apart from being a probably very irritating boy in her class, but to me she was the cleverest and prettiest girl in the world and her mere presence made me go all giddy. I can't help but think of her, even now, whenever I watch one of my favourite films 'Love Actually' – as the young lad Sam tries to explain to his father that 'the absolute agony of true love is just as real to a child as it ever could be!' Later in life, of course, we properly learn the difference between true love and a childish, pre-pubescent infatuation but she was the first of many (mostly unknowing) girls who would go on to twang my heartstrings in that 'agonising' way over the next decade or so!

One other friend I must mention before leaving Camborne, though, is James Kingston. Jamie lived down the hill from us in Dolcoath Road and his father ran a lawnmower supply and repair business from sheds in their back garden. He, and his brother Timothy, became friends of mine and Jamie and I used to go for long bike rides together, often taking a packed lunch and our swimming stuff before cycling off to Portreath. Even then Portreath was my favourite Cornish beach and I've already said I was to return there for family holidays year after year as an adult.

The beaches were something my dad particularly enjoyed about Cornwall – we seemed to visit a different one almost every time: St Ives, Carbis Bay, Newquay, Perranporth, Lamorna Cove, Marazion, Penzance, Gwithian, St Agnes, Hayle, Porthtowan…so many – and I'm glad to say we enjoyed them all. Well…maybe the time we were swimming at Gwithian Sands when the sea mist descended in minutes, turning a sunny evening into something of a nightmare, was merely memorable. While swimming in deep water the fret descended and, in what seemed no time at all, I couldn't see the beach – for that matter I couldn't see my hand in front of my face – and with dangerous rocks between me and the shore I had to rely on shouting voices to guide me back to safety. No wonder 6000 ships have been known to have been wrecked off the coast of Cornwall over the years – the combination of weather, mist and lethal coastline have seen to that.

The beach we frequented more than any other as a family though was St Agnes. This beautiful little bay has been somewhat overtaken by surfers and commercialisation in recent decades but, back in the early 1970s it was a quaint, old-fashioned little resort with little more than a car park, gift shop and an ice-cream kiosk. The sand was lovely and clean and soft and the cliffs protected the beach from most of the wind. Although dad loved going to St Agnes beach one thing he always tried to do was to drive there by a different route, often via tiny farm tracks that barely counted as roads – but that was dad to a T – he loved 'following his nose' and his amazing sense of direction rarely, if ever, let us down.

It was St Agnes beach that led to what was, most probably, my most embarrassing experience in Cornwall. On a beautiful, sunny day we were joined at the beach by friends and family from afar. The Lister family from Heckmondwike must have been staying with us along with my Uncle Keith, Aunty Doreen and their children (my cousins) Mary, Jason and Edwina. We had two tents in the back garden (one for the boys and one for the girls) as the adults had all our rooms in the Dolcoath Close bungalow.

My cousin Jason, Steven Lister and I decided to climb the cliff – as you do! It looks far more daunting in this photograph than it did on that summer's day, I can assure you! All was easy until the final step-up…a step of about 2 feet between the safety of the grass verge atop the cliff and where I stood several hundred feet above the beach. The naturally agile Jason and Steven had managed the final hurdle without any hesitation but, alas, I couldn't. Guess who had to be 'rescued' by the coastguard…oh dear!!

I've never been allowed to forget that little escapade – but there is so much more about Cornwall that I would never WANT to forget – nor ever will, for the county holds a very special place in my heart.

Two last photos of the 'Fortress' from 2015 including a 'salute to the past' in memory of many friends and influences at this 'so special' SA corps. The photos were taken shortly after the corps closed and became the Liberal Club. I hope the local community miss Camborne SA as much as I do. Pictured with me is my youngest son, Ieuan.

Chapter seventeen – On the English Riviera

Oh my! If beaches were one of our favourite places to be then the my father could never have chosen (with a little help, or more, from the Field Secretary) a better appointment than our next home – for in Spring 1974 we were appointed to Torquay – arguably the best seaside resort in the whole of the UK at that time. For us children it was beyond our wildest dreams; we were going from a smoky, northern wool mill town to the English Riviera via our two wonderful years in Cornwall. In fact, the night we moved – back up the A30 then across Dartmoor to Torbay, we left our boxed belongings and parked the car down near the seafront. There was a footpath specially built through trees, shrubs and rocks lit by coloured lights right opposite the seafront and we walked down that path as a family that first evening like over-excited holiday-makers….except WE WEREN'T holiday-makers – WE LIVED HERE!

My little sister Ruth stood in a bright red spotlight and, making reference to the town next to Camborne proudly announced, "Look at me! I'm Red Ruth!" Wow – we all thought…WHAT a place to live! Well…I may as well get this out of the way right now…to our eternal regret that first evening walking along the seafront as a family through those fascinating lights was the one and ONLY time we did that in the two years we got live in Torquay. How quickly we become accustomed to the best things that we are given – to the point where we hardly appreciate them at all. What fools we were – and how we felt the contrast when our next move took us back to the heart of industrial England, many, many miles from the sea…but that was still to come…

Torquay Citadel was a thriving corps in those days with a band of about thirty, songster brigade of forty, a large YP Corps and a healthy YP Band and Singing Company as well. The corps had its full quota of commissioned local officers and assistants and a very busy but effective corps programme in both summer and winter. A typical Sunday saw 2 open air meetings and Sunday Schools and three meetings including an afternoon Praise Meeting, something that was becoming less common even then. In the summer the afternoon meeting was replaced by an outdoor meeting up on Babbacombe Downs where we sat in chairs on a cliff-side lawn and held a full meeting with all sections, including timbrels, on duty.

After the Sunday Evening meeting the corps would form up outside the hall with a Police Escort to march through the town to the harbour, where yet another open-air meeting would be held on the Slipway. What an amazing witness that corps managed to sustain and crowds would flock to watch the spectacle and join in the hymn-singing. The Police Escort was needed because, in order to reach the slipway, we had to march the wrong way through a section of 'one way traffic' and, as all marching Salvation Army Bands know well – they have to obey the Highway Code!

Salvationists at Torquay Citadel were very aware of the legalities of marching and open-air ministry – and for very good reason! In the officer's room at the hall were two framed pieces of real Salvation Army history: photographs of some of the officers and soldiers of the corps who had been imprisoned during what became known as the 'Torquay War'!

PROSECUTED AND IMPRISONED
FOR MARCHING ON SUNDAY IN AN ORDERLY
MUSICAL PROCESSION,
TORQUAY, 1888.

When the Salvation Army first arrived in Torquay they took to forming a band and marching down the street, as all SA corps did around the country. It was a time of rapid expansion in the Army's evangelical activity and thousands upon thousands of souls were saved, largely from the huge numbers of alcoholics, addicts and prostitutes who were ostracized from the traditional churches and hitherto left unreached by the gospel. Torquay was the same – every Sunday the band marched and led a noisy, musical procession through the streets of the town. But the Torquay police tried to enforce local regulations that banned such processions on Sundays and, in January 1888 police arrested and charged the Salvation Army band with infringing these regulations. The Commanding Officer, bandmaster and several bandsmen were arrested, charged and fined but, refusing to pay their fines they were thrown into jail for their 'crimes'! In early February another eleven Salvationists were similarly arrested and charged.

Yet still they marched on! Every Sunday they led the procession and every Sunday more were summonsed – Salvationists even marched

all the way from Exeter and back to support those imprisoned and, again, to welcome them back when released! Over 100 soldiers were eventually prosecuted and Salvationists from 'nearby' corps like Exeter Temple, Newton Abbot, Crediton, Barnstaple and Ilfracombe often supported the local corps in the 'War' by sending soldiers in support. One of these, I have discovered in recent years was my wife's ancestor Fred Woolway (pictured). What an amazing way to link two historic SA families that Sarah and I should be so happy together - and Army - all these years and generations later!

Eventually, William Booth, the Founder of the organization became personally involved in the 'Torquay War' and so he sent his own daughter Evangeline Booth (later to be the Army's 4th General) to 'sort out the matter'. She was just 23 years old at the time. Her rallying words, upon arrival were, *"The majority in the world are sinners, and are quite against goodness, and I'm afraid it's the same in Torquay,"*

Evangeline Booth's high profile as a nationally known figure won the Army great local support and the 229 local Salvationists found their numbers swelled by many other members of the public – at times numbering 20,000 – and these sympathizers began to defend the Salvation Army as it marched the town's streets each week.

The 'Torquay War' went on for over six months before an Act Of Parliament was passed that, from that moment on, gave The Salvation Army the right to march the streets and hold open-air services wherever and whenever (obviously within reason) they wished. What a victory!

The framed Act of Parliament was the second item on the wall in that office and I spent many hours as a young boy looking at both of them, soaking up the amazing history of this organization I had been born into and raised up to be a junior member of. That same Act also gave women the same rights to preach as men – the first time in UK history such a declaration was made – truly a historic Act in many ways!

As the years have passed and bands have become smaller, older and far less inclined to march the streets and hold open-air meetings at all I find myself often immensely saddened that we have allowed to die such expressions of witness so hard fought for by soldiers of years gone by…but I'm happier to recall that in 1974 there were no such negatives in Torquay Citadel! The picture below shows Torquay Band in the open-air.

Chapter eighteen – Oh, no…He Wants Me To Blow My Own 'Trumpet'…

In my previous chapter about life in Camborne I mentioned playing cornet in the Stage Band for the musical 'Hosea' and hinted that that wasn't the end of the story…and so it wasn't. Torquay Citadel YP Band was a very good band, trained and led by YPBL Ken Parnell (he emigrated to, I think, Australia, later during our stay in the town).

Having seen me play in the musical and then, remembering that when mum and dad were appointed to Torquay, he had decided to make me welcome at the corps by buying a new cornet for me in preparation for my arrival. I have always had to try, like my father before me, to go the extra mile at times in order to not upset people unduly. Let me elaborate a little…In 2014 my youngest son (very much a 'mini-me' in many ways) was diagnosed with Asperger's Syndrome, a condition on the Autism Spectrum which often makes it hard to see the effect one's opinions and actions have on others. Because I and his 2 older brothers were involved in the diagnostic process the experts made efforts to point out that very similar traits had easily been observed in both of them and me – and from what I'd told them about my dad – even him too.

Although the two older brothers could (and should) have had the condition recognized and dealt with in their childhoods and adolescence it just wasn't known for such things to be looked for when I was a boy, let alone my dad in the 1930s – so we all remain 'officially' undiagnosed.

However, I now know enough about the condition that I am convinced that all of us would today be diagnosed thus (or something similar).

Dad often managed to upset people at times with unintentional comments or attitudes or, perhaps, by not recognizing in others a passion similar to his own but with a contrary opinion. I have been the same throughout my life and it has been a struggle at times to maintain relationships with friends and colleagues because of it. I know my mum often had, many times, to act as a peacemaker when this 'trait' had let my dad down – but, please believe me when I say he never had a nasty bone in his body…

I think, looking back on it now, both dad and I managed to upset Ken Parnell. I, certainly, had no intention of going back onto cornet 'where the veins stood out on my neck' and dad supported me. Rightly or wrongly, and no amount of regret can change the damage that happened more than 0 years ago, I refused to accept the cornet.

I was due to attend my first ever Summer Music School at Bruton (Bristol Division) in August and had registered as a tenor horn player; I had been practicing 'Swiss Melodies' as my audition piece with great dedication for many months but, as I dug in my heels, so did the YP Band Leader. He simply would not give me or try to find for me a tenor horn. My dad came to the rescue in the end by finding me one to borrow from nearby Brixham Corps which was, by then, a small enough corps not have a regularly functioning band. I played that horn at Bruton

160

and – I now see how much grace the YPBL must have had to allow this – I took my place in the YP Band on tenor horn in the corps.

All went well until December when Brixham Corps wanted to put a small band together to do some Christmas Carolling. They asked for the horn back and, of course, we had to oblige. I must admit I don't remember being unable to play during that time but there must have been a week or so during which I didn't have an instrument at all – and then, just as Christmas came, I received what was quite possibly the greatest Christmas present anyone has ever given me: The YPBL searched the little band cupboard at the back of the YP Hall and brought out a pitch black, tarnished and battered piece of metal. Telling me it was a euphonium he offered it to me, challenging me that "if you can get it to work" I could play it thenceforth in the YP Band.

The valves didn't work at all, the 4th valve was both cap-less and bent over double and as for tuning slides going in or out I dared not even try – yet 6 months later, at a Divisional Youth Event, I played 'Ransomed' and 'Song of the Brother' on that 'useless piece of metal' – two of the 'great' Salvation Army euphonium solos composed by George Marshall and Erik Leidzen respectively.

I have often heard my mum tell the story about the 'strange' Christmas in the Harry household in 1974 – for, instead of spending Boxing Day with the family watching TV, eating chocolates and playing with my haul from Santa the day before – I spent the whole of the day in the bathroom with my euphonium in the bath (no, not me as well!) with soaps and bubbles, washing up liquid and 'DuraGlit' silver polish, valve oil and Vaseline, pliers and polishing dusters responding to my challenge, "If you can get it to work".

With the water as black as the tarnished silver-plating had been I'm even told I left the instrument in the bathwater overnight. The consequence of this was that, even when my parents moved on from Torquay 18 months later, there was forever engrained on the bottom of the bathtub the shape of a euphonium that no amount of Vim, scouring powder or elbow-grease could remove! I can remember quite vividly bending the 4th valve back into alignment with dad's red-handled pliers; as I said it had no valve cap then as the old one had been snapped off inside the stem and it never did have one as I forever played it such as that it left a circular dent on the end of my left index finger!

I even received my first individual brass lessons since those I had had as a new beginner from Ron Taylor in Knottingley 5 years before – these from Ret. SL Bill Tout. His help, albeit for a short time, played a large role in my rapid progress as I began to savour the prospect of playing solos in front of other people and I thank him for his efforts in that respect to this day.

It must have been shortly after I made the transition to euphonium that I was, once again, invited to take up a place in the Torquay Citadel senior band. Torquay SA Band were, as I have said before, a very good band under the leadership of Malcolm Maddern – a man who became a good friend then and still is today, now living in Leicester and playing with the corps band at Leicester South. Among the pieces the band played I remember Norman Bearcroft's 'Just Like John', Eric Ball's Air Varie – 'Sound Out The Proclamation' and many others.

There were two euphonium players in the band, CT Peter Williams and Alan Luscombe, the son of the Corps Sergeant-Major Harry Luscombe. The 1st baritone player was Bert Ewing, then me and then Alan Marriott, an elderly Salvationist originally from Hinckley who was also a superb pianist. Whenever I visited Alan at home he would give me a piece of piano music to go away and learn, something that, as an aspiring musician I was, of course, glad to receive. As time passed young Alan Luscombe stopped attending the Army and so I was given the chance to sit next to Peter on euphonium. I loved it – but I hardly need to tell you that, do I?

I began to feature on Band Programmes as a euphonium soloist, although only 12 years of age, and I even received some invitations to play elsewhere. I guess I was viewed as some kind of 'child prodigy' back then.

Nº 7. IN EVIL LONG I TOOK DELIGHT

Solo for Euphonium B♭

Bandmaster G. MARSHALL

(My copy of the Euphonium Solos book was so old it still had the original title of the solo 'Ransomed' as 'In Evil Long I Took Delight'...I never was quite sure how 'long' that was for a 12 year old delinquent!)

My 2ⁿᵈ Music School was at Sunbury Court (what used to be the Junior National Music School by then, I think the West London Divisional School) . Major Robert Redhead was the camp Musical Director and other bands were led by BM George Mallion (Tunbridge Wells), Cliff Matthews (Gloucester) and, of course, BM Vincent Smith from Shildon. I attended this Music School for the next 4 years until 1978, it being very much a highlight of my year, EVERY year. That first year I made it into the 'A Band' under Major Redhead as 2ⁿᵈ euphonium to Nigel Barr and we played the Major's excellent suite 'Shout Salvation' from the original manuscript as our main work. I'm 2nd one in on the photo below next to my good friend Col. Neil Webb.

The whole saga as to how I 'arrived' on euphonium is so convoluted and, at times, absurd that I believe it has borne being told here – and I cannot believe such a story would have unfolded the way it did without God having a hand in the whole process. I had had no desire to play euphonium when I moved to Torquay in May 1974 but I have been proud to play that same instrument for the next 51 years as a soloist and with both Salvation Army Bands and some of the country's top Championship Section Contesting Bands as well. The euphonium and I were born for each other as far as I'm concerned! Thank you, Lord!

Chapter nineteen – More Memories From Torquay

Once again I have very vivid memories of the people I met at Torquay Corps, many of whom helped me so much as a young person, a young bandsman but, more importantly, as a young Christian. From the age of about 12 I seemed to be so busy with Army events that I had little time for much else. I was a pupil at Torquay Boys Grammar School although, to be fair, I did struggle with quite a bit of the work there and the high expectations.

At the end of our first year in the school our year group was split into 2 halves – the L group that made up 2L1 and 2L2 and the A group who made up 2A1 and 2A2. The 'L' stood for Latin and only the more able half of the year took Latin. What the 'A' stood for I never found out but it was 2A2 for me – bottom set in the bottom half of the year – but it was a top Grammar School, after all. Torquay Grammar school had an excellent reputation and the Headmaster Mr. Smith (known as 'Crunch' after Smith's Crisps) ran a very tight ship. I remember several of the teachers very fondly: Mr. Stokes was a kind, Christian gentleman who taught RE, Mr. Hopwood was the Music teacher (of course I'd remember him!), Mr. Rew taught me for both English and Art, Mr. Berry taught me History, Mr Liscombe Geography and Mr Thirsk taught us Woodwork and, I remember he drove a shiny, new Orange SAAB car.

There were two others I must mention – merely for the circumstances that surrounded them and remained with me through my own life and experiences in education later in life. Our Science teacher (I really cannot remember his name) used to sit in class sipping pure ethanol from a bottle via a teat pipette. One day he tried to show us how to use suction to make a vacuum in a bottle by sucking all the air out with some sort of condenser – he succeeded in sucking a large quantity of mercury out of a bottle and put the laboratories out of action for several weeks while they were once again made safe to use! He also showed us how dangerous acid could be – by dropping some deliberately onto the back of his hand and letting us all watch it bubble and blister for a few moments before neutralizing it by immersing his hand in a beaker of sodium hydroxide solution (alkali) he had prepared earlier.

In the last lesson before Christmas in our first year, while demonstrating water pressure with pumps and manometers he decided to 'have a bit of fun' by pointing the hoses at us pupils and soaking us all to the skin…on the day that Torquay saw its first snow in over decade (i.e. most of the pupils' lifetimes) and he was later blamed for several heavy colds over the Christmas holidays and suspended!

If he was a bit of a 'mad' professor then another teacher, sadly, did have problems of that nature and in a more serious manner. This was an elderly man who taught us English – albeit in a very slow, dry and old-fashioned manner. He was a very pleasant, polite and well-spoken gentleman however and, although I never actually had lessons with him I

did get to know him as I volunteered to help serve 'The Masters'
Dinners' in the Dining Hall several days a week. I did hear stories,
though, about how he often had no idea what his pupils were up to. One
lad, a Nigel Parsons, if I remember correctly, went to a lesson in disguise
and claimed to be called Cyril Nesbitt, causing the teacher to amend his
register. Cyril Nesbitt was a 'know-it-all' swotty type with a very
pronounced lisp and was to spend quite some time that day 'impressing'
the teacher with his apparently immense knowledge – including
'knowing pi to a million decimal places'. How? He recited random
numbers for nearly 5 minutes as the old man's face grew ever more
amazed! When Nesbitt failed to show for his next lesson Parsons told
him that the new 'star pupil' had had to leave again to help his father
with research into the 'Six Million Dollar Man' (a popular American TV
show of the day). On another occasion a tiny lad called Gubbins hid in
one of the lockers at the back of the room and spent the lesson coming
out with loud, random 'squeak' noises as the poor teacher searched in
vain for the source of the interruptions.

After some months that teacher left the school due to ill health
and the lessons were taken over by a different Master. In the following
December I went with the Salvation Army Band to a Mental Institute
called 'Star Cross', near Newton Abbot, to play a Christmas programme
for the inmates. My father, leading, noticed they had particularly
enjoyed the timbrels (girls with tambourines) and their display to the
march 'Christmas Joy' and he invited any of the residents who wished to
'come and have a go'. A line-up of residents each took a tambourine

from one of the girls and stood in a line, waving them as the band played part of the march once again. The utter shock when I looked across and saw the same English teacher with a tambourine in his hand has never left me to this day…

Several other teachers at the Grammar School made their mark on my life in various ways: Mr. Hopwood (Music) encouraged me and persuaded me to take up the trombone more seriously, joining the school orchestra. I also took part in the School Production of Gilbert & Sullivan's 'The Mikado'. Mr Stokes (RE) was a, kind, Christian man who seemed to know the entire history of the school going back for ever and he was the kind of teacher who would wander off the intended subject at times and entertain us with stories and school-related anecdotes– such as telling us that Arnold Ridley the much-loved actor who played Private Godfrey in Dad's Army had been a teacher at the school way back in 1917 after being medically discharged from his duties in WW1. Mr. Rew taught me for both English and Art – he was my favourite teacher – patient and encouraging and my mother always kept a framed painting of a heron in the sunset that I produced in his class and was painted on newspaper. I should also say there were other teachers at the school who I liked a lot less, although I shan't go into much detail here about them! Much of the school's discipline was enforced by prefects from the 6th form who seemed to delight in punishing us youngsters.

I remember two detentions well simply because of the written tasks I was given to do – to write two sides of foolscap on 'why taking my pen to bits and putting it back together again in Maths class is such fun' and another two pages on 'the sex-life of the ping-pong ball'.

Torquay Boys Grammar School was very much a rugby-playing school. PE lessons consisted of running and rugby in the winter and badminton and cricket in the summer. I was not a fan of either running or playing rugby (my interest in the latter game is usually no more than watching Wales in the '6 Nations' every February) but the punishing hills of the hilly sports ground in Shiphay had to be endured. I would return home with my PE kit (red and black hooped rugby shirt) caked in the 'red mud' that is so indicative of Torquay. My rugby career was very short – I rarely got picked for any matches but was 'thrown on' to get some experience in the last 2 minutes of an 'inter-house' tournament.

We were losing by 3 points when, by some freak of time and space, the ball suddenly came through the air in my direction about ten yards from the try-line. All I could see between me and a little taste of glory was the class bully Christian Donaghue, his long red hair flying in the wind and his broken teeth (no doubt the legacy of the fighting he was renowned for) leering at me. Somehow, I managed to run in his direction and, with the ball tucked under one arm I extended my other hand right into his face and dived over the line to gain the victory. As I celebrated this rare success I heard a familiar voice in my ear, "I'll ****ing kill you, 'Arry!" To my relief Master Donaghue never carried out his threat!

Plainmoor – the home ground of Torquay United football club – was barely a stone's throw from our home in Cary Park Road. When the club played evening matches (they frequently staged what would have been their normal 'Saturday game' on Friday nights at that time) the floodlights illuminated not just the pitch but in our back garden it became like daylight! While dad and I went to the match my sister Eira would play in the garden until long after 'normal hours' even on the dark winter evenings. Torquay were not a very successful team in those days (or indeed before or since – they are currently out of the football league completely) but, of course, I had favourite players and cheered them on win or lose. Phil Sandercock, the full back was my favourite player at that time for some reason, I seem to recall although the goalkeeper Mike Mahoney was excellent. My father actually cost Torquay his services!

Dad had to travel by train up to London one day and sat on the train next to a face that he instantly recognized – it was Joe Harvey the erstwhile manager of Newcastle United. Of course, they talked football all the way to London – dad had been a Youth Officer at Newcastle City Temple Corps back in the 1950s and had watched some of that club's all-time greats during the most successful period in their history and, eventually, their conversation turned to our local team: Joe asked my dad if Torquay had any good players he might be interested in and dad recommended he take a look at Mahoney, pointing out in particular his excellent record at saving penalties. A few weeks later Mike Mahoney moved from Devon to Northumberland and Division 4 to the top flight of English football. I wasn't best pleased with my dad at the time but, once again, his 'eye' for a good player had helped a young sportsman on his way to a successful career.

At that time the authorities and police had no problem at all with fans running onto the pitch at the end of a game to greet and speak to the players and I used to run onto the field at the final whistle to ask a player or two to sign my programme. I was able to see quite a few 'famous' names at the end of their careers dropping down to a lower level to continue a final season or two and, amongst others, I got the signatures of Welsh international Wyn Davies (playing for Stockport County), future PFA chairman Brendan Batson, Chris Balderstone and Alan Durban. Balderstone, of course, not only played Division One football with Carlisle but also was a test match batsman (and later umpire) before his tragically early death at 59.

I continued my piano lessons in Torquay with a dear old lady who lived just around the corner at the end of our road, in a house easily recognizable as the home of a musician by the wrought iron treble clef in the gate. Hilda Raith was one of the most patient and dedicated teachers I was ever privileged to study with. She taught both Eira and myself, and we both did our Grade One piano examinations with her. I can still remember the pieces I played for that exam – one was the Soldier's March from Tchaikovsky's Nutcracker – then I went on to do Grade Two and start Grade Three before we moved away. Mrs. Raith was the teacher who first introduced me to the music of Chopin as well, encouraging me to learn a few of the more simple preludes and waltzes. Sadly, however, in all the years since I have never come even remotely close to mastering the more complicated ones, let alone the Etudes and Polonaises!

Our home in Cary Park Road was near enough to Babbacombe and Oddicombe beaches that I, as an increasingly independent 12 year old, could explore them on my own and I used to go fishing off the little pier at Oddicombe, one day returning home with a two foot long garfish that I'd caught and had placed in a bucket. Sadly the garfish is inedible and absolutely useless except as bait itself but that fish still remains the pinnacle of my angling 'career'! Our neighbours had two small sons and an old Jaguar car painted 'strawberry ice cream pink' but my memories of the street itself are limited to what I've written here with the exception of one extraordinary story:

My younger sister Ruth had the tiny bedroom immediately above the front door in the house. She had been just three years old when we moved there and was approaching six when we left. Ruth had a good imagination and was often, in later years, to 'invent' imaginary friends to keep her company – I guess this was quite normal for a little girl who was 6 or 7 years younger than her older siblings. Nearing the end of our time in Torquay Ruth expressed concern for her 'little old lady', however, and when asked to explain what she meant she told us, in quite a lot of detail, about her 'regular babysitter': the old lady in a lace cap and shawl who sat in a rocking chair at the end of her bed knitting as she looked out of the window to the street below. Intrigued by the detail she seemed to be able to share about this 'lady' mum spoke to an elderly neighbour a while later, asking her who had owned the house before it was purchased by The Salvation Army. Mrs Godfrey had lived in the street all her life and was happy to share the answer to mum's question with her. An old couple had lived there, she said, until they died. He died first and she then remained in the house, spending the vast majority of her time sitting in a rocking chair 'in that little bedroom above the front door. "I can see her in my mind's eye right now," Mrs Godfrey continued, "watching us in the street from her chair wearing her shawl and little lace hat, doing her knitting..." Wow! Who could believe in ghosts??

Mum with myself, Eira and Ruth atop the cliff overlooking Oddicombe Beach

One final non-SA memory comes to me of an amazing pantomime my family attended at the Princess Theatre. I never saw so many stars on stage at the same time and, although only credited as 'Special Guest' the cast was led by the wonderful Arthur Askey – what a privilege to have seen this great comedian 'in the flesh'. He was joined by long-time comedy partner Richard 'Stinker' Murdoch (as Stinker the Tinker), Bernard Bresslaw and Peter Butterworth (both of whom I knew well from the Carry On films) and James Hayter (the voice of the Mr Kipling's cakes advert). Dad met Peter Butterworth while doing his 'pub round' selling the 'War Cry' one Friday

.

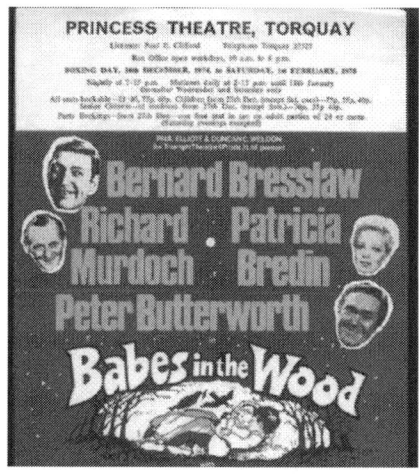

Dad also met Ronnie Corbett during our time in Torquay – I don't recall the circumstances, but I do recall dad being rather chuffed that the famous comic joked around with him – and even said that he reminded him of 'his big Ronnie'!

Chapter Twenty – More from Torquay SA

The Sunday programme at Torquay SA in the autumn, winter and spring was:

- 10am Sunday School/Open Air
- 11am Holiness Meeting
- 2pm Sunday School/Open Air
- 3pm Praise Meeting
- 6pm Salvation Meeting

But in the summer the 2pm and 3pm activities were replaced by a Corps Open-Air meeting up on the beautiful Babbacombe Downs. Chairs were laid out and one of the old pedal organs was used to accompany the songsters, played by Ret. SL Ernie Trethewey whose son, Terry was the corps songster leader. Both the senior and YP sections took part and hundreds of people used to come and listen, sitting soaking up the sun in deck chairs on the beautifully mown grass on the cliff-top overlooking Babbacombe and Oddicombe beaches. After the evening meeting during the summer there was, however still one more activity to complete, a march from the hall right down through the town – as I mentioned earlier a police escort was needed for as the route involved marching the wrong way down a one-way street – but we marched all the way through the town and down to the harbour slipway where another open-air service was then held. When the timbrels played the crowds would flock around us and people would join in the service right the way round the harbour. It was a wonderful experience and, looking back now, it was amazing how hard Salvationists worked on a Sunday at that time…I also find myself asking if we have gone too far in the other direction nowadays?

Then there were summer midweek activities as well. The band would play on the lawns opposite the main beach in Torquay, Tor Abbey Sands, fairly regularly. I particularly remember one such occasion when the band played an excellent programme including 'Neath Italian Skies', 'Sound Out the Proclamation' and Norman Bearcroft's 'Just Like John'. After such concerts I remember we sometimes went in for a quick swim before going home – absolute bliss…usually! On one particular occasion I remember that the weather turned a bit nasty after our concert ended but my friend Nigel Boulton and I were determined not to miss out on our swim! So we went for our dip in the pouring rain and with enormous waves crashing ten feet or more high! We read the next day that a young man had been killed or seriously injured swimming at the same time when such a wave threw him against the stone steps…so maybe we had a lucky escape there! Thank you, Lord!

Nigel's mum, Jean, was our Singing Company Leader. I remember us persuading her to let us 'add drums' to the singing company songs so we found an old drum in a cupboard somewhere and painted it a bright, shiny red. The only problem was that neither of us could play it – my drumming skills are still awful now so goodness only knows what a terrible racket I inflicted back then, probably ruining the singing company's efforts. At least my eldest son Morgan has gone on to become an excellent drummer/percussionist – and he has played on several CDs with bands and songsters as well as performing with Championship Section brass bands. He didn't inherit THAT skill from me!

The YP and Youth activities at the corps were excellent, as I have perhaps suggested by mentioning the YP Band and Singing Company activities – but also there was a thriving group of Corps Cadets and the Sunday Schools had a very large attendance, swelled by mini-buses that picked up many children from a nearby council estate. I have many memories of happy coach trips to Youth events in Plymouth or Exeter – we would wave at a local 'celebrity', the tramp 'Smokey Joe' who lived in a lay-by near Exeter on Telegraph Hill and, sometimes we even stopped and gave him a cuppa from a Thermos flask and some sandwiches.

I even got my first proper 'kiss' on one of those coach trips, even if it was only the result of a 'dare' – it didn't matter at all that she was Nigel's girlfriend and not mine…wow…I think I saw stars!

Sheila Stanbury was the YPSM whose job must have veered between Christian educator and crowd-control most of the time. How she oversaw all of us as well as looking after her own 4 children must have been some feat but, as always, I can't help but thank God for the patience and dedication of all my Sunday School teachers through the years. They had a lot to put up with!

My parents always looked back on their time in Torquay with some mixed feelings for, although we made many great family friends that we stayed in touch with for many years and dad went back on several occasions to conduct funerals for some of them, there were some problems in the appointment that led to health issues, particularly for mum, whose health throughout the 1970s was rather fragile. I won't elaborate on this topic further but, even as a 12 year old, I was aware enough to realise that one person in the corps was making life very difficult for them and, when I got married many years later mum only asked me one thing – and that was not to name any children I might have by that man's name! I don't think she needed to have worried!

Dad always loved his pub rounds and he often recalled a story from the Torquay days later in his life. He loved a bit of banter and, one Friday evening, as he stood with his collecting box in hand in one pub near the harbour, he was watching the darts players keenly. As they repeatedly missed their target he joked that they weren't doing very well and one of them turned round to him and said, "I suppose you could do better, could you?" and handed dad his darts. Dad, who loved playing darts himself, took them and hit the bullseye with his first attempt, much to everyone's amazement (and probably his own as well)!

From that day on whenever he walked into that bar the players would take his collecting tin and papers from him and one of them would go around collecting while dad had a quick game of darts with them! The only problem came when 'Farewell Orders' came from the Army and we all moved away from Torquay. The new officer innocently walked into the same pub but was greeted with "Where's our big Welsh bloke?" Having tried to explain that their big Welsh bloke now lived in Stoke-on-Trent the disappointed darts players removed the 'little Irish bloke's' cap...and poured a pint of beer over his head! Oops!

Other things that happened during our stay by the seaside included dad joining the Rotary Club – he remained a loyal Rotarian for the rest of his life – and he was invited to preach at the Rotary International Conference in Torquay in front of thousands of people, the largest congregation he ever addressed...a very proud occasion for him.

Less well-received was the colour-scheme he chose for the redecoration of the Army hall and corridors. I don't recall every detail but I know two of the colours used were purple and lime green (well, it WAS the 1970s...anybody who lived through the decade must be embarrassed by some of the wallpaper we used to live with!)

Visiting sections to the corps during our time in Torquay included Cardiff Canton Band and Songsters, Hendon Songsters and Upper Norwood Songsters, both of whom sang in the splendid surroundings of St Luke's Church up on the hill overlooking the harbour.

The Upper Norwood visit almost didn't happen. Lots of the liaison and planning for the weekend was done between dad and the Upper Norwood Songster Sergeant Barbara Wellman (who was a close family friend of ours). She told us how the Songster Secretary had tried to book a coach to bring the songsters down and had been shocked at being quoted several thousand pounds…it turned out that the coach company had misheard her pronunciation and had quoted the price for a coach to Turkey, not Torquay!

What I DO recall, most vividly, about those weekends, though, was the consistently brilliant music presented by each section – Hendon Songsters particularly standing out for me. Upper Norwood, though, had that lovely friend Barbara Wellman with them as Songster Sergeant. Barbara had visited our home a few times as an always-welcome guest and her recitations (I'm sure she preferred the term 'elocution') were a special highlight on that occasion. I'm not sure if she did it on the songster weekend but I have precious memories of her reproductions of some of Joyce Grenfell's famous 'George…don't do that!' sketches. Barbara was a headmistress and the only drawback to her visits in our house was her constant reminders to Eira and I to make sure our homework was done!

Also, having mentioned dad's problems with the hall redecoration it was interesting to overhear a conversation between him and the vicar of St. Luke's who had, similarly, recently received criticism from his bishop about the renovation of his church. I still giggle today as I picture his face as he impersonated the prelate opining, "What have you done? You've turned my church into a discotheque!"

Cardiff Canton Band was led by another close family friend, BM Leslie Young. Les had been in the band at my father's home corps Cardiff Stuart Hall and his father, Ernie, had been the BM in those days. Dad, as well as his brothers Trevor, Owen and Peter had all been in the band and I know how unhappy dad was when Stuart Hall had to close in the mid-1960s after a compulsory purchase order was made on their hall. Officially, Stuart Hall was to merge with Cardiff Ely corps (and it became known as Ely Stuart Hall) but, in reality, most of the corps soldiers moved to the various other corps around the city. My grandparents, their sons Trevor, Peter and daughters Dorothy, Gwen and Gwyneth all moved to Cathays but a lot of others swelled the ranks of Cardiff Canton, still today the Army's largest presence in the Welsh capital.

I can remember Ernie always being in the congregation when we visited Canton with his pristine white epaulettes as retired BM, while Les acted first as Ivor Bosanko's deputy BM and then took the band on after Ivor moved to the USA. Both Les and Ernie took me, as a young boy, to Ninian Park to

The Salvation Army
Torquay Citadel
Band Weekend Festival of
Sounding Brass
by the CARDIFF CANTON BAND
(Bandmaster: Leslie Young)
Saturday 20th March 1976 at 7-30 pm
in St. Luke's Church (off Abbey Road)
Guest Ticket

watch Cardiff City and I have remained a 'long-distance fan' of the club ever since.

Another of dad's printed programmes (produced oh his old Adana printing press), this time for the visit of Canton Songsters

A few years ago, when Les Young was Promoted to Glory, Sarah and I were privileged to be part of the band at Penarth Corps that played for his funeral. Amongst other memories I have of he and his dear wife Maureen (Mo) was being invited to their house to watch England v Brazil in the 1970 world cup – in colour!

Just a week or so before we left Torquay the band went away for a weekend visit to St Ives in Cornwall, where our old friends Major & Mrs Bob Davey were the Corps Officers. It was the first 'away weekend' the band had undertaken for quite a few years, I believe and I was thrilled recently to find the programmes for that visit.

Saturday Evening

Song	696	Tune 591
Prayer	F. King	
Festival March	The Scarlet Jersey	R. S-Allen
	Introductions	
Selection	Jesus Folk	Larsson. arr R. S-Allen
Song	Go, Tell it on The Mountains	Male Chorus
	Caroline Cornish at The Piano	
Cornet Solo	Someone Cares	arr R. S-Allen
	Soloist: S. Ldr. T. Trethewey	
	St. Ives Section	
Song Arrangement	Sing Hallelujah, Shout Hallelujah	Camsey
	Announcements & Collection	
Suite	The Pilgrim Way	Ball
Devotional Period	Testimony G. Ward	
	It took a Miracle	Male Chorus
	Bible Reading B. Sgt G. Hann	
	Selection The Day of Grace	R. S-Allen
	Courtesies	
Air Varie	Sound Out The Proclamation	Ball
	Benediction	
Finale	Temple 85	Bearcroft

Song	690	Tune 198
Prayer	N. Boulton	
March	Minneapolis (iv)	Soderstrom
Introductions		
Selection	Eine K'eine Nachtsmusik	Mozart. arr Jakeway
Euphonium Solo	Song of The Brother	Leidzen
	Soloist: Bandmember Marc Harvy	
Elocution & Organ	Bandmember Christina Stanbury	
Selection	Youth's Ambition	Bowes
Devotional Period	Testimony	C. Treasurer Williams
Song	I Know Whom I have Believed	Male Chorus
Bible Reading	C. Turner	
St. Ives Section		
Announcements & Collection		
Selection	His Guardian Care	R. S-Allen
Courtesies		
Festival March	On Parade	Herikstad
Benediction		

In addition to the pieces seen on the two festival programmes above I can remember that the two devotional meetings were based around one of my father's favourite bible stories – the occasion when Jesus appeared to the disciples on the road to Emmaus after His resurrection. There are two band pieces that are based on that story: Ray Steadman-Allen's 'Emmaus Journey' and Dean Goffin's 'Road to Emmaus' – and the band played one in each of the morning and evening meetings.

I did a lot of 'growing up' in Torquay – and in many different ways – as a sometimes frustrated student, a young musician and performer on both piano and euphonium, as a young Christian, and, not least, in learning to accept that sometimes I would 'fall' for a young lady and get absolutely nowhere! That last one was to be an ongoing lesson for many, many years to come for I was never going to be the sort of lad who had girls queuing up for my attentions…oh boy, no! *(But I HAD had that one kiss!)*

As always, at the end of the two year period, the 'envelope' from National Headquarters must have arrived sometime in April and our house once again became full of boxes and trunks; our precious belongings were packed away, mum's china ornaments and plates meticulously wrapped in triple thickness sheets of The Daily Telegraph and carefully placed into the trunks and, once more, it was time to say farewell to friends both at school and the Army – for the Harrys were 'on the move'. A week later we discovered that we were moving to the industrial North Midlands, the 'Potteries', Stoke-on-Trent. It was only when the stark reality of our new location began to sink in that we started to realize that we hadn't really taken advantage of our beautiful seaside location as much as, perhaps, we should have. That first evening walking amongst the lights by the promenade remained the ONLY time we did that during our stay in Torquay…and days on the beach were soon to be days that would only happen on annual holidays – for Tunstall was well over 50 miles from the nearest coast.

And so we bid 'adieu' to Torquay although it is a place I have always regarded fondly. I was to return many years later for band contests (Torquay is the home for the West of England Area Championships) and even for short holidays but, sadly, I have no friends still there with whom I ever kept in touch.

Like Camborne, it was sad to watch from afar the decline of the corps (at least numerically) over the next few decades although it has been more pleasing to hear of good things happening there in more recent days, especially since the return to the site of the hall that had to be left for many years. Structural damage, caused by industrial excavation, left the hall site unfit for purpose and the army had to 'move in', by necessity, with a local church for quite a number of years.

Some corps folk moved elsewhere and it has been nice to meet up with them from time to time. Peter Williams, Terry Trethewey and others moved to Exeter Temple and, having married into an Exeter family, I have met some of those over the years and my old BM Malcolm Maddern and his family moved to Leicester – I billeted with them when the Portsmouth Songsters went to Leicester Castle corps many years later and we have met more often since I moved up to Lincoln. Malcolm wrote a Christmas Medley for the Torquay YP Band that contained a beautiful euphonium descant to Away In Manger that I have continued to 'add in' for over 50 years now. Thanks Malcolm!

Chapter Twenty-One – I'd never even HEARD of Tunstall!

What did I know of Stoke-on-Trent? To be honest, not a lot! Like most places I only knew of its existence because of the football team Stoke City. I knew of them, of course, with their famous red and white striped shirts and badge with a sort of 'fat chimney' on it. I could recite the names of the players in that team with no problem at all: John Marsh, Denis Smith (the commanding centre half who had broken almost every bone in his body for the sake of the game, or so I'd read in 'Shoot!'), John Mahoney (Welsh international, no less!), Alan Hudson, Jimmy Greenhoff, Alan Bloor, John Ritchie, Terry Conroy (who had scored the winner in the League Cup final against Chelsea a few years before) and, of course, the great Gordon Banks! But as for the PLACE, the district and its history I knew nothing at all. Happily, that was to change very soon, and the affection with which I grew to love Stoke-On-Trent over the next three years (yes – THREE – for the first time ever!) has stayed with me for a lifetime!

After Torquay, with its golden sand and palm trees, Stoke, at first, seemed rather bleak. A 'black', smoky town full of ageing factories with red brick and dark, glass windows, grey roads and streets – and grey skies too, for the sun seemed to not shine through the cloud quite as brightly – well, at least, at first! That was to change very soon, of course – for this was the famous 'summer of 1976' – by far and away the best summer of weather in my lifetime if you like it hot and dry!

We arrived at 17 Queen's Avenue, as always, on a Thursday afternoon to be welcomed by the elderly Home League Secretary, Evelyn Poulson, and a nicely prepared tea in the dining room of our new house. The thing I remember most, apart from her being in full SA uniform to perform her little duty, was the wallpaper in that dining room for it was the most lurid, almost luminous bright green and was patterned with one of those 1970s designs that had a similar effect on the eyes and brain from what I'd imagine LSD to be like! The house had three large rooms downstairs as well as a kitchen and 'outhouse' and a paved-over back yard with a few sorry-looking shrubs and a wooden access gate to the lane behind the house. Upstairs, there were four bedrooms and a bathroom and steps to an attic that had been properly floor boarded. That this attic had an electric light and power supply as well pleased this young lad as it immediately became a wonderful play-space for my Scalextric set!

What I didn't see, of course, was the crack at the front of the house that was caused by subsidence or a few other problems with the house – why would a young, carefree teenage boy have his attention caught by these? But I do recall a LOT of decorating by mum and dad and new furniture being purchased for the 'quarters' quite soon after our arrival. We also had a laugh at home when dad told us about the paltry sum DHQ had offered for the said new furniture and the reply from the Corps Census Board to the Divisional Commander asking him where they might purchase furniture made from 'orange boxes'!

Photograph of our family in front of 'that' wallpaper

Tunstall Hall, in Ladywell Road in those days (1976-79), I remember as a wonderful place. It reminded me straight away of an old theatre or Music Hall (which, indeed, it had once been) and it had what seemed like endless rooms and areas to explore! The main worship hall had a slight slope from back to front and a large platform – ideal for bands – and my dad took full advantage of that, booking visits for Enfield *(below)*, Hendon, Chalk Farm and Bristol Easton Bands to visit for weekends during the next three years.

A large gallery looped right the way round (with, I seem to recall, the remnants of a now removed second gallery/circle above that – though I may be mistaken…). The band room was under the platform and reminded me of a damp old cave and it, too, had its own hidden alcoves where, from time to time the BM would reach in and produce a blackened old tenor horn or cornet that I used to assume had been there since before William Booth started shaving! Steps from the side door led to a kitchen and then up to the YP Hall and there were more stairs again up to the gallery and 'glory shop' – a large space used mainly for storage but had also been, at some time, a thriving youth club.

Tunstall Corps had a very proficient and large band that played very well indeed under the careful, skilled and dedicated eyes and ears of BM Don Perry. My initial sadness in the corps was that, after 4 years of playing 'full-time' with the senior bands at Camborne and Torquay, I was NOT to be allowed to play with Tunstall Band until I was made a Senior Soldier. Being, in May 1976, 5 months short of my 14th birthday that meant a frustrating wait to join them – but I was, at least, allowed to attend senior band practices as well as YP Band ones, of course. SL Ron Coombe led a fine brigade of songsters and there were thriving YP sections with 20+ in each led by SCL Betty Perry (the BM's wife) – although Don jr. (their son) was Singing Company Leader for a short part of our stay at the corps before he moved to Scotland. Ray Newton was the YPBL and his assistant was Howard Paskin - one of several Paskin brothers at the corps. The Sunday School (YPSM Kath Hall) numbered 60 or 70 children and workers – Tunstall was, by far, the largest corps I had ever been part of - and I loved it! 'Proper' Army!

There was also a thriving Home League and an Over-Sixties club with two lovely, older chaps sharing its leadership. Bram Pollett (also Ass. CSM) and Eddie Williams always made me very welcome when I popped in to entertain the old folk during my school holidays (more of that later…).

There were two meetings every Sunday and there were also two Sunday Schools, as was the case in most corps at that time: the morning Sunday School being very much Bible-based while the afternoon meeting helped us to understand what we were part of – The Salvation

Army - with its own particular beliefs and characteristics. It is my belief that the loss of this aspect of our children's ministry in the last forty years has been at least partially responsible for a large part of the decline in both SA children's ministry and also the organisation as a whole: several generations of youngsters have now grown up not knowing what a 'senior meeting' is like until well into their teens and never had the opportunity to learn what things like the doctrines, uniform, flag, crest and other SA characteristics are all about – how we became the Army we are (were?), learning 'our' songs etc.. I completely understand that these things are far less important than teaching children about the love of Jesus and encouraging them to accept Him as their Saviour but, along with the almost total demise of Corps Cadets in the UK, it is not uncommon in these days of 'one meeting per Sunday' for young people aged 17 or 18 years of age to know almost NOTHING about what they are supposed to be part of – and then we wonder why they feel excluded and often leave.

Maybe I was part of the 'other extreme' in this argument, inasmuch as I could have recited the names of all the SA Generals in chronological order before I could quote lengthy passages of scripture but I was, with my friends, well-taught about Christian principles and grounded in the faith I have nurtured ever since. It was this that instilled in me my yellow, red and blue blood – it is WHY I believe in The Salvation Army and its unique place and ministry within the Christian Church. I have watched my own children grow up in the army in more recent years and the emphasis and ethos they have shared with me about modern SA Youth work growing 'young Christians' as opposed to the next generation of Salvationists has ultimately led to most of them and their friends now worshipping in other churches, if at all, while the SA continues to decline in numbers in the UK.

The photos and article here are from the local newspaper after I had returned from my summer music camp with the 'top student' award and trophy.

BOY WINS TOP MUSIC AWARD

A top National Salvation Army music award has been won by a 15-year-old North Staffordshire boy.

Euphonium player Marc Harry, a member of Tunstall Salvation Army Corps Band, was presented with the trophy for the most outstanding musician in the annual boys' music school for brass staged in London.

And it was a case of fourth time lucky for Marc, who is believed to be one of the youngest winners of the Evangeline Larner Cup.

He has entered the event for the past four years, and on the last two occasions was awarded third place.

The only son of Major Kenneth Harry, officer in charge of the Tunstall Corps, and his wife Jean, Marc faced fierce competition from more than 100 other young Salvation Army musicians from throughout Britain during the week-long school, which involved written as well as practical sessions.

A pupil at Stanfield High School, Marc, of Queensavenue, Tunstall, was short-listed in the top eight possible winners of the trophy before the final decision was made.

Very proud

Said Mrs. Harry: "We were in London when the final festival was held, and we were able to see the cup presented to Marc. We felt very proud of him. It is quite an achievement."

And Marc, who intends to take part in next year's music school, told the Sentinel: "I was not expecting to win the cup. I was surprised. I have been going for four years, and I have gained third place for the last two years. The school is for young people under 16, and I think I am one of the youngest to have won the award."

Chapter Twenty-One – The Senior Corps

Of course I would never have admitted it back in October 1976 but I guess all the evidence shows that I became a senior soldier shortly after my 14th birthday primarily so that I could join the senior band. A great many of my friends up and down the country did exactly the same – and this is a thing that is very largely frowned upon today and regarded as a 'bad thing'. I am not so sure it *is* all that bad... My own dad told me that he arrived one morning at Cardiff Stuart Hall for the meeting and was ushered into the Officer's Room with,

"Come in here, quick, Ken, and sign this – you're being 'done' this morning!"

...and that was the first he knew about it. So my preparation lessons were, at least, a bonus he never had in the early 1940s. My senior soldiership lessons were shared between my mum and Brigadier Reg Hayman, a retired Welsh officer who lived in nearby Hanley. Reg and his wife were very, very dear to us as a family and they became 'surrogate grandparents' to Eira, Ruth and I for the three years we lived in Stoke. Mum and dad had been fellow officers with them during their days in South Wales and through the Aberfan disaster written about in an earlier chapter. Brigadier Hayman enrolled me as a senior soldier in October 1976 and I was as proud to be made a soldier then as I ever recall being proud of anything up until that point in my life.

I have to admit, though, that the erstwhile Brigadier was a '2nd choice' as I had always expected to be made a soldier, when that time came, by Commissioner Albert Mingay. In a meeting I had been in with my parents back when I was a *very* young child the Commissioner had delivered the sermon and I had repeated every word of his sermon as he spoke under my breath and into my mum's ear – maybe some very early practice for one day delivering sermons of my own! The Commissioner and his wife had visited Torquay as 'specials' and the decision for him to enrol me apparently came about then – but, sadly, Mrs Mingay's health had declined too much by 1976 for him to come to Stoke – and, hence, that task fell to Brigadier Hayman. Commissioner Mingay did, however, send me a signed book, "God in the Slums (The story of Hugh Redwood)" as a gift to mark my enrolment – a book I still have today, of course.

I am not sure if I was then allowed to take my place in the band or not, although I suspect not, as the rule then was that you had to wait three months after enrolment as a soldier to 'join the sections'. I do recall that I still played with the YP Band for the duration of our stay in Tunstall but I was, finally, allowed to leave the singing company on my dad's strict understanding that I joined the songsters instead! Betty Perry allowed me to choose the singing company song for my last Sunday as a member and I chose Joy Webb's 'Light Up The Sunshine', thus ending my 10 years in the singing company that had begun, aged 4, in Bargoed.

In my first songster practice I felt very 'grown up'. My voice was still in the process of 'breaking' or getting deeper at that time, so maybe 'bass' wasn't my best choice on that day and I went home with a rather sore throat. If this is 'confession time' then I have to admit that I didn't enjoy my initial few songster practices although I duly became a songster, as expected. The extension to that confession is that, over 40 years later now, I have NEVER regularly enjoyed songster practices very much in all that time (although they have been a bit better since I became songster pianist – around 1998 at Portsmouth). I still don't enjoy them a lot today – but that is neither a reflection of the many excellent Songster Leaders I have served under in that time nor despite the fact that my rehearsal frustrations have been a small price for me to have paid for the opportunities of service that being a Salvation Army songster have given me over those years. I wish I knew why I have found songster rehearsals such a difficult experience – for I have enjoyed singing and playing for the songsters in meetings and festivals a great deal…maybe it was just all those endless Thursday evenings when I couldn't wait for the weekend to get here...?

With the band we did 'away weekends' to Hollinwood, Royal Tunbridge Wells and Letchworth, where I remember my grandad Harry driving up from Cardiff to see us on the Sunday afternoon. Solos I played with Tunstall Band included Ray Bowes' 'Song Of Triumph' (I was later to record this solo with Portsmouth Citadel Band on the CD 'Journey Through Time') and Ray Steadman-Allen's 'The Ransomed Host'. I sat third euphonium in the band most of the time below Kevin Mowbray, the band's principal euphonium, and Cyril Lockett. Cyril was a lovely chap – I remember he was 53 at the time as he pointed out that his age was the number in the tune book we were playing. He had a fine, but (by then) slightly old-fashioned euphonium sound with which he regularly contributed to band selections but I remember him most for his vocal solos – 'O What A Wonderful Day' being his favourite testimony to sing during open-air services.

Kevin, brought up in Hednesford Corps, was the principal euphonium player in the band and he was the first man I ever knew to have a Sovereign euphonium, a brightly shining, silver-plated new model produced by Boosey & Hawkes. How I wanted one of those – but my Imperial model did just as well! Kevin used to play Leidzen's 'Song of the Brother' and Ray Steadman-Allen's 'The Conqueror' as his solos of choice at the time. He usually featured on Saturday evening programmes and me on Sunday afternoons!

198

Several photographs of Tunstall Band in the late 1970s. BM Don Perry and the whole band in an open-air meeting – and (below) in a festival you can see Kevin Mowbray and Cyril Lockett (my fellow euphoniumists) and many others.

Regular items on band programmes included 'Portraits from St Paul's Epistles' and the newly-published 'Variations on Laudate Dominum' by Edward Gregson. Devotional selections, however, were where this band truly excelled and the warmth and sincerity they were able to convey through such pieces as 'The Penitent', 'Wonderful Healer' and 'Hill Of Calvary' will always be my 'benchmarks' for how effective such music can be in presenting the Gospel through Army banding. I recall how one bandsman had been 'out' of the band for several years but, unknown to anyone but himself, he had taken to creeping into the foyer at the front of the hall on Tuesday evenings just to listen to the band rehearse. It was while his fellow flugel-horn player Eddie Williams played the solo in 'Hill of Calvary' one Tuesday evening that Roy dared to come into the hall, kneel at the Mercy Seat and rededicate his life to God and Army banding. Sadly, although Roy was able to resume his place in the band on flugel horn, further subsequent health problems were to eventually curtail his service.

Despite all the good playing, however, band programmes really came 'alive' when the band sang. I can only recall three songs they ever sang – and only one of them was from a SA publication, being perennial favourite 'It Took a Miracle'. The other two were sung, I think, on every programme I ever did with the band – and, from what I've been told, that period lasted a good while longer than the three years I was with them! 'The Bend in the Road' was a close harmony song that was always popular but 'A Little Talk With Jesus' was real 'barbershop' stuff and guaranteed to raise a smile!

Sometimes we regard a teenage (or young) life surrounded by lots and lots of Salvation Army activity as being a bit 'sheltered' but that doesn't always apply. I did quite a bit of 'growing up' of another kind one evening while out with Tunstall Band! We were playing in a church somewhere out in the countryside and, as was often the case on such occasions, a local politician, celebrity or businessman had been invited to be 'chairman'. Now, while I was taught that the first requirement of a good chairman is to put a large donation in the collection plate (my dad's 'slightly tongue-in-cheek' philosophy) the general consensus is that a good chairman will tell a few good stories and describe the music in the concert without a) talking too much (most fail!) and b) without embarrassing anyone (including himself!). This particular chairman was a local musician and, despite being in a church and also having a Christian brass band to compere he decided to neither adhere to any expectations we might have had nor be in any way sympathetic to the band and its evangelistic intentions – for he proceeded to fill the evening with ever more lewd and filthy anecdotes about the famous conductor Sir Thomas Beecham! I had heard of Beecham but had no idea of his reputation for being either very blunt or grossly and graphically rude...but I did by the end of that night! I think we were all very embarrassed and nothing was said about it all the way home but try as I might I've never forgotten some of those stories!

And that brings me to one of my favourite stories that I learned from 'The Potteries'. The great man Josiah Wedgewood was one of few names associated with the area that I could ever have recalled hearing of before moving there. My dad was told a story one day, on a visit to the Wedgewood factory, and it was a story he was to retell many times over the years to come. It was about a young lad, an ancestor of the story-teller I recall, who was brought to Wedgewood's office on his first day at work. Wedgewood asked a works foreman to 'show him around' the factory. The foreman had a bit of a reputation for his bad language and inappropriate topics of conversation, so Wedgewood himself made the point of following them around a few times during the morning to check on the boy's welfare.

In Wedgewood's office was a particularly striking old vase, very beautiful and, obviously, worth a great deal of money. The great man had known that the works foreman in question greatly admired this vase and, at the end of the tour, he invited the foreman to visit him again in his office. Carefully, the great man lifted the vase and, in a gesture of apparent thanks to his worker for showing the boy around, he held it out to the man. But, as the foreman reached out his eager hands to take the precious object Wedgewood dropped it, deliberately, onto the hard floor, watching it smash into a thousand pieces. The foreman, shocked, swore again and asked Wedgewood why he had done this, for he would have paid everything he earned to have owned it. Wedgewood told him that he could go into the pottery and make another vase, just as beautiful, again – but NOTHING could now be done to repair the damage his 'dirty talking' had done to corrupt that young man Wedgewood had placed into his 'care' earlier that day. The foreman learned a great lesson and never acted in that way again.

Although the chairman for that concert, as far as I know, never heard that story nor realized the impression he had made, unintentionally or not, on my young mind that night, I'd like to think that he might have had the opportunity to reflect on his folly in some way at some point in his future like that works foreman.

I mentioned in an earlier chapter how my father used to like doing 'something different' for the Harvest Festival from time to time (remember the Harvest of the Sea at Camborne, for example?). At Tunstall, one year, his latest idea was to hold a 'Harvest of Flowers'. It was amazing – I have never seen such colour and such a tremendous array of flowers as we saw in that occasion. At the centre of all the flowers that completely filled the front of the platform was a full-size replica painting of Holman Hunt's famous 'Light of the World'.

This masterpiece had been painted by a local man whom dad had met whilst visiting. He had knocked the door of one of the families from the corps and a neighbour of theirs opened their door to inform dad that they had gone out. As was his way dad engaged them in conversation and, a few minutes later, he was invited into their house for a chat and a cup of tea instead! Their house was like an art gallery, for the old man who lived there spent his time reproducing famous paintings – there was the Mona Lisa, The Haywain and, of course, Holman Hunt's most famous work too. As a result of that visit we were able to borrow the painting for the weekend and, afterwards, the man's wife started attending the Home League.

Dad had an effortless way of communicating with ordinary people in an extraordinary way. That last story was just one example of this and another also came about during the years we were at Tunstall. One of dad's friends from the Rotary Club became very ill with cancer and was near the end of his life. What upset the man's wife more than anything else was that she did not know how to make his last days in any way enjoyable or memorable – he was just a sick man who had lost all his enthusiasm for life and barely spoke, even to her. He simply lay in bed waiting for the end to come. That was until my dad visited! Dad had always loved cameras and photography, as I've mentioned before and, it turned out, so did this gentleman. Within minutes of dad's visit the dying man got out of his bed and fetched from a cupboard bags full of cameras, flash units and tripods and the pair of them chatted and enthused together for several hours.

The man had spent his whole life working for Royal Doulton and so, while they chatted together on that and several subsequent visits, his wife and my mum (who knew each other from Inner Wheel meetings) spent their time looking at some of the porcelain treasures that they had accumulated during their time together. One piece, in particular, caught my mum's attention. It was a Royal Doulton bone china teapot in the shape of a camel being pulled to its feet by its Arab owner – glazed white but decorated in striking gold. Unfortunately, its lid had broken, but all the pieces were there. In time, after several such visits, the man passed away and dad was asked to conduct his funeral service, which he did.

His wife, in gratitude to my dad for his friendship and for helping to brighten her husband's final months, gave the cherished teapot to my mum as a gift and it remains, to this day, a family treasure. I can find little or no reference to such a teapot online despite my own quite extensive research on the internet – I hope, one day, we might have the chance to take it to something like the Antiques Roadshow – I suspect it just might create something of a sensation for I have a strong feeling that it just may be a unique item!

Wherever he was stationed as a Corps Officer my father's 'flock' was the whole town, as these and many other stories illustrate. He tried to walk down the High Street in his uniform nearly every day, available for people to approach and talk to – this was his special personal ministry and one he relished to the very end of his life. In retirement, when he had lost a leg and relied on his mobility scooter, he still rode from home to town most days, engaging people as he went. When dad was Promoted to Glory in 2002 my mum went into their local undertakers to book his funeral and the response from the proprietor was one of disbelief: 'Not Ken – it can't be – he was only in here talking to me and bereaved clients on Friday?' That was my dad all over.

Chapter Twenty-Two – The YP Corps

The YP and Youth of the corps performed the first musical that I had been a full part of since 'Take Over Bid' at Tunstall – the musical in question being 'Jonah Man Jazz' – and I was chosen to play Jonah. Whether this was the first time I'd been properly expected to sing vocal solos or not I can't say (I know I HAD sung solos before but only as 'one-offs') but I can remember enjoying the experience and wanting to do more of it!

In the photo above I am in the centre (with rather 'damp' armpits!). My two sisters Ruth and Eira are also there, of course, and many friends who we have been privileged to be able to stay in touch with in the years since. On the back row are two of the Paskin brothers, Howard and Donald – Howard was Deputy YP Band Leader. YPSM

Kath Hall is behind Ruth on the left and her daughter Carol is behind her. Julie and Ruth Perry, daughters of Dep BM Geoff Perry (later BM and now PTG) both became Salvation Army Officers – at the time of writing Major Julie Rowley (nee Perry) is the corps officer at Chesterton with her husband Julian. Two of the other boys seen here, Nigel Jervis and Jim Bailey, were also schoolfriends of mine.

My main solo in the musical was the 'laid back' "I Need a Boat, Man" and that is me singing it above while other members of the cast lounge by the 'waterside'.

As well as playing with the band, YP Band and singing with either the Singing Company or Songsters we had a thriving Corps Cadet Brigade at Tunstall. It was on a Corps Cadet weekend that I was asked to 'preach' my first ever sermon – and I still have my typewritten notes from that talk in my study bible today!

One of the highlights of our stay in Stoke was when the YP band was invited to an event that was to be graced by the presence of HRH Prince Charles (Now, of course, King Charles III). We rehearsed for weeks; the timbrels were meticulous in their deportment and drill and we all had pristine, ironed white shirts as we set off in a coach for the special day. The sun shone, the school where we set up was so tidy it must have been sterilized! The walls were freshly painted, the paths weeded, the lawns manicured so carefully. And we played. And the timbrels waved.....And Prince Charles walked in completely the opposite direction and missed us out entirely! The photo below shows YPBL Ray Newton leading the band at the event.

The two young ladies playing trombone and cornet in the picture were also school-friends of mine as well as friends at the Army. They were a year above me at school but we were all part of a very, very fine school orchestra at Stanfield High School on High Lane in Burslem. Hilary Coombe (now Sharp) played the trombone and she played violin in the ensemble. I (along with Art teacher Mr. Light and a few others) formed the orchestra's trombone section. Jacqui Wallbanks (now Kilsby) who is playing cornet in the band photo played timpani in the orchestra.

Our music teacher and the orchestra's 'maestro' was Bertram Capey and he managed to produce exceptional musicianship from a perfectly 'normal' secondary school orchestra. We played many local concerts and church services, did radio broadcasts and won the 'Open Orchestra' section First Prize at the prestigious Alderley Edge Music Festival playing Walton's 'Crown Imperial' march. There must have been about 70 of us in the orchestra – my sister Eira learned to play the oboe and every part was covered, including a couple of bassoonists.

Knowing how hard it is today for whole cities like Portsmouth (where I did most of my own teaching) and even some counties to put together a full orchestra shows the tragic decline in music education in our schools over the past few generations. At that time we used to have two full weeks 'off school' each year to go and have intense musical training at the Wedgewood Training Centre in Barlaston. Guest musicians would come in and teach us – but, much more importantly, INSPIRE us during the day and then, in the evenings we would go to concerts or the theatre. The cost of such a week today would be frightening and far beyond the reach of any ordinary state school. How grateful I am that governments of those days invested more wisely in education!

STANFIELD HIGH SCHOOL ORCHESTRA'S CHRISTMAS CONCERT

Playing for parents and pensioners

Hilary was the daughter of the Corps Songster Leader and 'top trombone' Ron Coombe (her Grandfather Jack Beckett also played trombone in the senior band at the corps). She and I also played piano duets on YP Band programmes and I remember teasing her mercilessly during our rehearsals for these (sorry, Hilary!). If it's any consolation (probably not!) I only teased so to cover the fact I'd have actually quite fancied her and would've liked for her to have been my girlfriend – but I was FAR too shy to have even considered asking back then, as anyone who knows me will understand!

Chapter Twenty-Three - Some Personal Recollections of Stoke Folk!

When I think of the corps-folk of Tunstall so many of them stand out in my memory – and for all sorts of reasons!

The real gentleman who probably had the biggest influence on my life in the corps at Tunstall was the Corps Sergeant-Major Peter Worthen. Peter, although you would never have guessed it if you met him away from his daily work, was a Coal Merchant – a coalman, as we would have said back then. He spent his working week lugging hundredweight sacks of coal from his wagon to the coal bunkers of houses right around the district – yet you would never see him at the army or on any other occasion with the slightest hint of black under a fingernail. He was as immaculate in his appearance as his life reflected the Christian values he lived.

I was often privileged (yes, I DO call it that!) to be invited to go out on his rounds with him during school holidays. I learned how to collect the coal from the depot, filling the sacks and lining them up on the lorry, jumping out of the wagon when parked on the weighbridge – then Peter would take me into the café for '2 fried eggs on toast' before we started the round. Strangely, we didn't wash our hands before eating the said meal, but I'm sure the coal dust made it taste better anyway! Peter would tell me about the different types of coal we had 'on board': best Welsh anthracite – the most expensive but slow burning, dense and of the highest quality – right down to the recently imported Russian coal that he disliked rather intensely – mostly dust and rubbish, but considerably cheaper and soon to herald more and more pit closures in the UK.

Then we'd be 'on the road'. At first I was only allowed to carry the smaller half-hundredweight sacks but I soon persuaded Peter to let me try the 'proper' ones and we carried coal from lorry to bunker for the rest of our working day, arriving back at his beautiful detached house and gardens several hours later absolutely shattered – and absolutely BLACK! Then he would press a crumpled pound note into my hand…my first paydays! What a thrill for a young lad! We kept in touch with Peter and his lovely wife Eunice after we moved away from Tunstall, visiting her after Peter's Promotion to Glory some years later and my dad spoke to them both on the telephone very regularly – usually as part of his Sunday Evening marathon phone session (he would ring many old friends and family on Sunday evenings when he got home from the Salvation Meeting).

The photo above shows CSM Peter and Eunice Worthen with their great friends Dinsdale & Win Pender when all were official delegates at the 1978 International Congress held at Wembley. Although I was not able to be at all the Congress celebrations there are many things from it that stand out clearly in my memory. The West Midlands Divisional Youth Band took part in a Festival in the old Wembley Conference Centre with the Seoul Boy's Home Band from South Korea and we heard them play the wonderful piece 'Faith Reborn' that had been composed for their visit by Major Les Condon.

Then, a few days later, we returned to London for the final weekend of the Congress. I decided to play the role of 'roving reporter' and, armed with my dad's cassette recorder and a microphone, I walked between many different events 'capturing the atmosphere' and interviewing anyone who looked remotely important or interesting about their Congress experiences and then asking them to send a message back to some of the aged Tunstall comrades who were unable to be at the congress (I remember later making copies of the tapes for some of these comrades like dear Harry Dobbs).

What I have on those 3 hours of cassette tape is an amazing memoir of the event – I had interviews with Salvationists from all around the world – names that read, at times, like a Salvation Army 'Who's Who'. There is also, of course, a lot of wonderful music – sometimes in the background but also in the forefront!

Another thing I remember doing for the first time whilst at Tunstall was entertaining the Over-60s club with music and funny stories. I was regularly invited by the TWO Over-60s Secretaries Bram Pollett and Eddie Williams to give up an hour of my time in the school holidays and go to entertain the club. The shows I did all those years ago formed the basis of a ministry that has continued for my whole life – they became the 'One-Man Variety Shows' that I still take to many corps around the country all these years later. The shows have 'evolved' somewhat since those early days, of course, but some of the items I used back then still resurface occasionally even today!

One such item is the 'Old Tyme Piano Medley'. This concept I find rather fascinating, in fact…for what was 'Old Tyme' in 1977 is positively ancient in 2025! I find it a little hard at times to reconcile the fact that today's octogenarians grew up with Elvis and The Beatles and not Hoagy Carmichael and Cole Porter! So, me playing a medley of 'I Wonder Who's Kissing Her Now', 'Stardust' and 'As Time Goes By' is more likely, today, to elicit memories of the listeners' parents than their own past! This does mean, however, that a Beatles medley is now able to be part of the show – something I'd never have even considered playing for OAPs back when I first started!

There are several school teachers from Stanfield that I remember most fondly, at the forefront of which must be Mr. Rainbow. Geoff Rainbow was my French teacher but he also sang with the school choir, played viola in the orchestra and ran the chess club, of which I was a member. He was such a kind, patient man who managed to inspire me to a top-grade O Level pass in French despite having little or no interest in the subject at all. Because he often did a lunch duty his school dinner was brought to him on a tray during the first lesson after dinner-time and

he would sit eating it while teaching us. This led me to give Mr. Rainbow's classroom the nickname 'The Multi-Coloured Slop Shop' (in reference to a

223

popular children's TV show at the time).

What a delight it was for me many, many years later to find Geoff Rainbow (above) again on Facebook! By then of course, he was long retired from school teaching but still teaching languages privately to students and preaching on the Methodist circuit. He was also a singer in the Keele Bach Choir and still took delight in sending me his incredibly detailed programme notes that he always wrote for their performances! I travelled to Stoke a couple of years ago for this lovely gentleman's funeral service.

Another teacher, who tracked me down through the internet many years later, was Tricia Gilbert. Mrs. Gilbert taught me English and Geography and she would have been amongst my youngest teachers at that time. She told me recently how, as a young, inexperienced educator, she often dreaded teaching my class. How rude! Well, apparently, there were two of us in the class who filled her with trepidation. This was in the days where in school reports each pupil was given a 'class placing' for each subject and Kieron O'Hara and I vied each other for top place in every class. If he was first, I was second and vice versa – almost without exception. At least it must have meant we were trying hard! But poor Mrs. Gilbert also knew that, if we were in the classroom, every single slip she made in spelling, punctuation or fact would be picked up on and she told me her poor heart would sink whenever she saw mine or Kieron's hand go up in the air! What an insufferable little brat I must have been at times – ha-ha!!! Despite this, she assured me that she regarded the two of us very fondly amongst her recollections as she reminisced in her retirement!

Mrs Gilbert even got a fond mention in a poem I wrote several years later jokingly bemoaning my teenage years:

I Hated Being a Teenager!

I hated being a teenager!
It wasn't too much fun, I say
To go through all that growing up
Thinking I should win a cup
For being the coolest dude around
And you think your own voice is a wonderful sound...
Face of zits and hairy armpits...
I hated being a teenager!

I hated all that 'falling in love'
And spending weeks in misery;
You thought she was a lovely thing
But whenever you asked she gave you the fling.
Then – she went out with your best mate –
Who turned from a pal to an object of hate.
Classroom lambs...
And then EXAMS!
I hated being a teenager!

I hated when nobody bothered to hear
The things you thought were helpful.
No-one took you seriously,
They acted all imperiously
Then whatever happened was always your fault

"Cos you just didn't think and your head's full of bolts"
It's not fair!
AND I WANT LONG HAIR!
I hated being a teenager!

I hated going on first dates,
Nothing ever went right!
Fifteen baths and then a shower
All in that last half an hour
Then, when you meet her make up's wrong,
You hate her perfume – awful pong!
Always behave!
And having to shave!
I hated being a teenager!

I hated being off my food
When taken for a ride:
I learned the meaning of a song called 'Joy'
From an album by Nilsson I'd bought as a boy...
Kay was my 'Joy' – my confidence wilted
Twice I went back and was twice more jilted
Early to bed
With guts like lead –
I hated being a teenager!

I hated all that 'go to bed'
When something you like's on TV!
One pair of boobs and the tutting starts –
Why ARE we embarrassed by bodily parts?
Gorgeous Tracey Barratt's were pert,
I saw them when they tumbled out of her shirt!!
A schoolboy grin,
Is it a sin?

I hated being a teenager! (but it had its moments!!)

I hated Mrs Gilbert too!*
(Don't think she liked me either).
She taught us for English and boring Geog
With a face like a lemon and a voice like a frog
But most of the teachers were not too bad
(And poor Mr Allen, they drove him mad...)
Mr Plant was a 'weed'
And Ridgeway? Indeed!
I hated being a teenager!

I hated finding the years had gone,
Ne'er a teenager again.
I woke up one day and found I was twenty,
From having no worries I now carried plenty.
My friends were dispersed, and
What was worst –
The youthful bubble I'd had had been burst!
And now I'm a man
I carry the can!
Please can I be a teenager again?

*Of course I didn't really! She was a great teacher who helped me gain another two good grade O levels! Poetic license, it is!

My two best friends at school were also Salvationists – but not at Tunstall Corps. Paul Dale and Paul Critchley attended Smallthorne Corps (now incorporated into Stoke-On-Trent Corps). We were utterly inseparable both in and outside of school. Paul C was known as 'Soggy' and so Paul D and I became 'Doggy' and 'Oggy' in turn. We even formed a little school brass band and taught our Maths teacher Mr. Clark how to play euphonium so he could join in with us! Soggy played trumpet and Doggy the tenor horn and we spent every lunchtime and break singing or playing something or other in a practice room or behind the curtains on the stage in the school hall. We were doing so one day when an impromptu school assembly was called and we sat in silence as we heard the pupils gather below. I can't recall the exact detail but somebody in the school had done something they shouldn't have and the Deputy Head, Mr. Johnston, obviously decided he needed to address it.

However, as he harangued his silent audience a certain trombone player (ahem!) suddenly had the bright idea to stick his trombone slide through the curtains right over Mr. Johnston's head! There followed rapturous laughter from the amused students – so he (I) did it again…and again. Fortunately for me he never did find out what was amusing those he was trying to reprimand, or I fear a far greater reprimand may have been heading my way!

Doggy (Paul Dale) and Soggy (Paul Critchley) outside Smallthorne (now Stoke-on-Trent) SA Hall in 1979.

Paul Dale has remained one of my closest friends throughout my life. He is still a Salvationist and is Songster Leader at the Stoke-on-Trent Corps. His younger sister Tracey (Mountford) is a Salvation Army Officer. Paul Critchley is very well-known as a Worship Leader and he is the founder of Presence Worship in the same area. We were reunited a while ago at Mr. Dale senior's funeral. Mr. and Mrs. Dale never missed sending cards to me and my children every birthday and Christmas – ever – and, even now, they come from another daughter!

I 'worked' for the first time in Stoke (not including coal delivery) – firstly, I had a paper round that enabled me to save enough pennies to buy a bike and a decent stereo 'music centre' – the latter on Hire Purchase from the Co-Op and I remember cycling down to the Co-Op on 'payday' to give them the latest instalment towards my acquisition. Then, later, I got a job some evenings and school holidays at a small pottery – 'Staffordshire Potteries' had two buildings on opposite sides of the town. Mostly, I worked at the one nearer to where I lived. The pottery made nothing but 'reproduction antiques': plates for hanging on a wall, massive Aspidistra Pots, china dogs, Toby Jugs and chamber pots – but, mostly, those little, round, porcelain plaques onto which transfers of classic prints were placed; then they were re-glazed, mounted on velvet and put into a gilt frame. My job was the least glamorous – putting a 12 foot piece of frame into a cutter, pushing down a pedal with my foot and, hence cutting out a 90° notch that would allow four pieces to be stapled together to make a frame. How boring that assignment could become when practiced for a whole day I will leave you to imagine! The proprietor of the pottery, Paul Singh, a little Indian man with a goatee beard was not interested at all in alleviating my boredom – but he did give me the money for which I endured the task.

I seem to remember so much about those three years…such as playing cricket on the fields behind Paul D's house for endless hours during the summer – and what a summer 1976 was! I played football and basketball for the school teams – with and against some who went on to become famous in the professional game like Mark Chamberlain and Adrian Heath. These were the years in which I began to explore the world of music outside the realms of The Salvation Army, classical music and even pop music – indeed I discovered Harry Nilsson, who remains my favourite musician ever today!

Even this love of Nilsson's music came about because of The Salvation Army! Dad was collecting from the shops in town for the 'Sale Of Work' – a sort of Autumn Fayre that most corps held each year selling goods that had often been made by Home League or Ladies

Fellowship groups as well as other, assembled bric-a-brac and items. A record shop in the town had given dad two LP records and dad, knowing how much I loved listening to multifarious types of music, had bought them himself to give to me at Christmas. One was the soundtrack album to a Spaghetti Western with music by Ennio Morricone - and the other was the soundtrack to a very obscure film for a movie that was never even properly released in the UK. I've never seen it on any TV channel, you can't get it on video, DVD or BluRay and it is not even known if a good quality copy of the film exists at all today!

But the music for the film was composed and sung by Harry Nilsson and the film starred the singer himself and someone else I'd only vaguely heard of called Ringo Starr. The 'cowboy' soundtrack, though still in my record collection nearly fifty years later, remains largely unplayed but the Nilsson album literally changed my life for ever! Over the next few years I bought (or had bought for me) everything the great singer and songwriter ever produced and, in 2001, I organized the International 'Harryfest' for fans at the Hotel Russell, London, which was attended by Harry's son Zak and many others including Hollywood & TV actor Curtis Armstrong who remains a good friend today.

I studied piano with Chris Yates, who lived just a few doors down from us in Queen's Avenue. Chris was a former 'child prodigy' who had been a concert pianist in his teens and recorded several LPs. Then, in the 1960s he had been in a pop group who had become a 'one-hit wonder'. With the proceeds from this he had bought a very posh car but he still lived in the same terraced house with his parents by the time I knew and studied with him. However, he still had a dual-career and recorded pop music under the pseudonym of Kelvin Mattheson.

I wrote my first 'official' song with 'Kelvin'. I had always put together silly little ditties but not what I would call a proper 'song' then I took a simple effort called 'Prove Myself To You' to my piano teacher who added far better music to it than I had - and he recorded it to use in a series for which he was providing music for BBC Radio in Ireland. I wish I had a recording of it! I remember getting such a thrill hearing 'my song' played and sung by a professional – and it inspired me to write more! Sadly, some years later, and after the deaths of his parents who Chris both lived with and adored he took his own life. I still have an old cassette of one of his songs, the chorus of which meant so much to him (and to me):

"Without music there is no tomorrow,

Without music, I would surely die."

So, my song-writing began – and, at the time of writing this book I have composed 315 songs. They are, by all means, not all good, and many were neither written down nor recorded and, thus, have been forgotten forever – but there are, of course, others that are used and sung in many places around the world today. Now and again I look through an old journal or pile of old school books and find more scribbled lyrics from a long-forgotten effort and a long-forgotten melody will flitter across my memory. If that seems a waste then please, believe me, the best and most usable songs – as well as a few of the others – have been, or are in the process of being, recorded for posterity!

The next two songs I wrote, though, were love songs…and the full story behind their composition is one for another day and another book, perhaps… Suffice to say, for now, that the ups and downs of a shy teenager falling madly in love and discovering new, unimagined ways of being terribly and excruciatingly hurt had absolutely everything to do with their composition. I often wonder what happened to my 'muse' at age 15. Kay Bloor played second violin in the school orchestra and was a couple of years younger than me and the six months or so that she dominated my thoughts and dreams affected me for much, much longer than that – for my fragile psyche and self-confidence with girls was truly shattered for ever…I didn't/couldn't ask another girl out for over 9 years…

Those two songs, the first 'The Way of the Stars' quickly followed by the (better) 'Love You Til Eternity' proved popular with my friends and I was endlessly asked to play and sing them during breaktimes and lunch hours at school. They even get an airing now and then in my concerts all this time later.

Then, in May 1979, my parents received their Farewell Orders once more and the family prepared to move up to Northumberland – to an old mining town called Bedlington that was about 14 miles north of Newcastle-Upon-Tyne. I, however, still had O-Levels to complete – so the rest of the family moved without me and I was left in the capable hands of Bill and Jean Lamplough, Salvationists from nearby Chesterton Corps. This was my first taste of living 'away from home' but Bill and Jean certainly did their very best to make their home mine and I was looked after for those next 6 weeks or so extremely well indeed. Bill was a very fine euphonium player himself (his son and grandson have gone on to be bandmasters at Birmingham Citadel, one of the finest Salvation Army Bands in the Territory) and grandson Gavin (the current BM) is also principal cornet with the International Staff Band. One of the first things Bill did was make sure I practiced my euphonium – and, to encourage me, he lent me his hand-written copy of a (then) unpublished Erik Leidzen solo 'Home on the Range'. I was later to get and often play the version published and was rather surprised, if not a little disappointed, that this was a little easier than Bill's original!

Bill and Jean went to London one day for a big SA event – this was, in fact, the Royal Albert Hall festival of 1979 commemorated by the excellent double LP 'Song of Exultation' – and Jean had left instructions about the meal that she had left in the oven on the timer. When the time came for me to eat the aroma from the kitchen had most certainly whetted my appetite and I went to the oven. What happened next left me with a brand new dilemma – for inside the casserole dish was the biggest piece of perfectly cooked beef I had ever seen! I NOW know that this was a rather generously sized 'steak' but my initial thought was that this couldn't be MY tea alone! Surely, this was also tomorrow's Sunday joint?

We ate beef at home but not very often. I have stated many times before that for Salvation Army Officers in the 1960s and 70s money had to be stretched as far as possible! Most Sundays we had a chicken or some pork. If we had beef, which was in those days more expensive than other meats, then it was a very special treat. Mum would cook the joint the night before so that dad could carve it cold and, hence, in thinner slices so that there might be enough left over for another family meal on Monday. This 'steak' I had before me was, indeed, larger and much, much juicier than ANY beef joint I had ever seen cooked at home! Was it really ALL for me to eat? I had no-one to ask and, needless to say, it was utterly delicious – although I was still expecting a reprimand the next morning if I'd eaten the Sunday roast!

The reason I had stayed behind in Stoke was, as I wrote above, O-Levels! These (or the slightly easier CSEs) were the exams we all took at the age of 16 - the culmination of 11 year's schooling in the UK.

I was taking 9 O-levels in English, Maths, Chemistry, Physics and Biology, French, Art, Geography and something called 'General Studies'. This last one we had absolutely no 'special' preparation for and didn't really know what to expect until the day we arrived for the exam!

There were two papers - one like a General Knowledge quiz with multiple choice answers. Having been brought up in a household where everything from 'Ask the Family' to 'Mastermind' was watched avidly I had little problem with this one. I guess it was a test of how 'rounded' our education was; whether we were just classroom 'sponges' taking in what we were told by teachers or whether we learned 'outside' the classroom as well.

The second paper required us to write two essays on topics chosen from a given list. I ended up writing pages and pages about, first Black Dyke Mills Band and then about 'Star Trek' which I had grown to love as a TV series (I'm old enough that it was, of course, the original series back then with Kirk and Spock).

No music, I hear you all ask? Well...no, for I had been told that Grade Five practical and theory Music passes counted as the equivalent of an O-Level and, having passed both of these before the 'options' were offered at the end of the 3rd Year (now Year 9) I didn't see the point!

Walking across the 'greenbanks' on the way to my Art practical, near the end of my exams I passed some Port Vale players doing some training with their coach. To my utter delight I recognised the coach as the great Gordon Banks - a legend of the 1966 World Cup Final (it was the only year England had won it...and still is!) I gratefully received a precious autograph to add to my collection - actually signed on my O-Level Art prep sheet!

I spent a lot of time during these last few weeks with Paul D Paul C (Soggy and Doggy) revising (a bit), entertaining the Smallthorne SA Over-Sixties Club and playing cricket outside the back of the Dale House in Duddell Road. Happy, happy times indeed.

Chapter Twenty-Four – Howay, Man – We're Geordies - A Difficult Move

First of all, I had never even HEARD of Bedlington! Secondly, the three years we had lived in Stoke-on-Trent had been amongst the happiest of my life (I had never lived ANYWHERE for three years before!). I also had to leave behind the best and closest friends I had ever had. It's safe to say that this was the hardest of all the moves for me, personally.

One of the first things my parents and sisters experienced in their new home was a Salvation Army youth 'Field Day' – in which the youngsters from all around the Northern Division gathered to compete in races, football etc. for a day. I received from home a full and detailed description of the massive success that Bedlington SA had on that occasion with winners' names highlighted in the programme and an overwhelming sense of excitement about how wonderful the next stage of our lives were going to be. There was a massive youth presence in this corps they described to me that they assured me I would 'love' as soon as I got there…there was also a great and very loud band that I would LOVE playing with…and there were OVER SEVENTY singers in the Songster Brigade!

Yet, I could not muster much enthusiasm about saying goodbye to Stoke's dirty old pot banks and leaving Soggy, Doggy and all my other friends behind in the Midlands as I swanned off somewhere vaguely 'Up North'! Besides, Stoke City had just won promotion back to the top division and my season ticket was itching to be renewed! Could I ever feel the same way about Newcastle United (who had recently gone in the opposite direction down to Division 2)?

So many questions and so many conflicting thoughts went through my mind in those days and weeks that I remained in Stoke after my family had moved to their new home, yet I knew I would have to follow them in time and, before too long, that day came. I went back to school one more time to say my goodbyes – and then it was time to leave.

On arriving in Bedlington, which felt like it was on the other side of the world at first, I found we were to live, once again, in a council house on a large council estate called The Hartlands. Our house was on one of the longer sides of a rectangle with a large field of grass in the centre. It was a good enough house although not as big as our last quarters in Tunstall - but it did have that large field in front and a garden at the back that actually had some grass (Queen's Ave, Tunstall had had a concreted 'back yard').

Another real 'downer' was the fact that, having thought I'd left school (Stoke schools had a '6th Form College' system in which school was left behind and 'grown up' education began), Northumberland 6th forms were still part of the secondary school – so I was having to go back to school with more 'little 11 year-old kids' again! EVEN WORSE, my new school was not only six miles away in Morpeth but they actually wore SCHOOL UNIFORMS there! I hadn't worn a school uniform since I was 12 at Torquay Grammar!

How could I possibly settle with all this going on? I began, for the first time, to experience what my sisters had gone through several times – a difficult 'Officer's Kid' move – and I didn't like it at all. I sat in my own bedroom quite a lot that summer, I recall, listening to my records until I was almost bored with them. So I joined the local library – one that lent records as well as books. That single event changed everything for me!

Let me explain…

My family had often gone 'specialling' in the past. That is another Salvation Army 'word' that means going away from your home corps to lead a weekend at another, usually involving a concert on the Saturday evening and the then leading the usual Sunday services. As a family we were quite well suited to this additional branch of ministry, Mum and dad sang duets (and I could now accompany them on the piano), I could play euphonium or piano solos, Eira played oboe and sang with a lovely contralto voice and my younger sister Ruth performed some recitations in a most amusing fashion with her little personality bursting through even then. The whole family could play brass quartets (cornet, horn, trombone and euphonium) and sing in 4 part harmony together.

The family had done two of these away weekend visits in 1979. The first had been in February earlier to Newbiggin-By-The-Sea on the Northumberland coast – just 6 miles from the place we were now calling 'home', although, at the time we went there, we had absolutely no idea that was what lay ahead just three months down the line! If Bedlington was going to be as cold as Newbiggin had been (I recall an open air meeting in a terraced street when the freezing wind blew straight off the North Sea most profoundly) then it seemed another good reason to stay safely in my bedroom!

The other weekend away before had taken place just as my parents moved from Tunstall to Bedlington and we visited Hemel Hempstead in May. I remember playing Leidzen's famous euphonium solo 'The Song Of The Brother' and 'Someone Cares' on the Saturday evening and then went to my 'billet' with a family called Norrie who were part of the corps there. I rarely, if ever, got nervous playing euphonium solos although I recall having just a little trepidation when my dad told me before the festival that evening that one of the best euphonium virtuosos in the world was sitting up in the gallery...

I had not long arrived at the Norrie household when the telephone rang and, most surprisingly, I was told the call was for me. Who could be calling me in somebody else's house? When I answered the phone it was no other but that great man Barrie Perrins himself calling me to congratulate me on my playing and to give me enormous encouragement to continue my progress. That phone call remains today a highlight of my life. How kind of him to bother to call me like that. Many will tell you that Barrie was a true Christian gentleman, yet he was denied the opportunity to serve God through Salvation Army banding because he played with contesting bands – that was how he came to be a Salvation Army Soldier but one who sat in the gallery each week rather than with the band. I am so glad we have changed that particular regulation in more recent years!

And so I continued to practice – but now even MORE keenly thanks to Barrie's encouragement. That was one massive change in my musical life from that weekend. The other came about as a result of the Norrie's son, Paul – a lad of a similar age to me. I have already written about my love of the music of Harry Nilsson and (this shows how much I still had to learn about the world of pop and rock music in 1979) Paul listened to my musical tastes without too much interest until I mentioned the collaborations Harry had recorded with someone called Ringo Starr.

"What? Ringo the Beatle?" Paul asked…but I had no idea! I had HEARD of The Beatles, of course (I even remember hearing the news of their break-up on the TV news while we lived in Heckmondwike) but I didn't 'know' The Beatles or their music at all. Paul began to put that right at once, playing me his records for the rest of the weekend.

It was only natural, then, for the first record I borrowed from Bedlington Library to have been 'The Beatles 1962-1966' – the 'Red' Greatest Hits collection. I played those four sides of vinyl over and over again, getting to know the songs and learning to love them like new friends (maybe to replace the ones I'd left behind in Stoke). Within two years I could have gone on 'Mastermind' answering questions about The Beatles, its members and music. I devoured The Beatles like a starving man might devour bread: records, tapes, biographies, magazines, newspaper articles…literally anything I could get my hands on to feed this obsession. When dad visited DHQ in Newcastle one day and returned with 2 old electric guitars donated to the Army for youth work I grabbed one, asked my mum to teach me my first three chords then didn't stop practicing until I could play every Beatles song in the book. By December 1980, just 17 months later, when John Lennon was killed, I knew most of the group's solo output as well.

Yet the majority of the music in my life, even then, and still today when my tastes have diversified far, far more than they had then, was the music of The Salvation Army. Music that I had loved, heard and played most of all in my life – and I thank God for that every day!

A pencil drawing I made in the front room at the Hartlands house that summer of the centre picture from The Beatles' Sergeant Pepper album.

Chapter Twenty-Five – Bedlington SA and the 'Wow!" Factor

By the time I arrived in Bedlington, about six weeks after the rest of the family had got there, there was a lot of uncertainty in my head – and for someone who was usually fairly self-confident and assured that didn't help me feel any better. I had, of course, missed the 'welcome meeting' and, while my parents and sisters were already feeling quite settled and could put names to faces I was, for the first time, WAY behind them! The only person I'd met before was the CSM Brian Storey who had been the 'chairman' for our family concert in Newbiggin a few months earlier. Brian, an accomplished musician and music teacher himself, had, at least, let the corps-folk know that this 'ageing, teenage ex-prodigy' was on his way and, therefore, I wasn't going to have to work my way up from 2nd baritone again! I was given a 4-valves up at the top Yamaha euphonium, as seen in the photo below, and given a good welcome.

There were, indeed, over forty players in the band and more than seventy in the songster brigade: both sounded like the 'massed' forces I had experienced previously in ensembles I'd been part of where several corps joined together for special events! The songsters, in particular, could sing so powerfully! The men sang with a passion I had never encountered before, as if from the very depths of their souls – men like Norman Dixon, Jim Wearmouth and the BM Jim Burn projected powerful voices that made the fire of the Holy Spirit a raging inferno that burned itself into your very soul! Some of the ladies could match them, too – Nancy Jobson powered the contraltos with a 'baritone tenor' range with her own voice projection every bit the equal of the men I just mentioned!

Yet, when they sang, this battalion of voices was immaculately controlled by the gentle expertise of SL Eric Burn (son of the BM). A controlled pianissimo in the wake of 'Richter Scale' registering fortes nearly blew my mind. THERE, in a nutshell, was this 'Wow!' factor – and within a very small space of time I was not only 'at home' in the corps but very, very much 'in love' with it!

It was with Bedlington Songsters that I first sang some of the beautiful songster music published by The Salvation Army at that time: Ivor Bosanko's classic arrangement of Herbert Booth's 'I Bring them to Jesus', William Himes's 'Filled With the Joy of the Lord', John Larsson's 'The Living Waters' and many more – but also, to sing long-established 'classics such as 'My Treasure' (Ann Sage/George Marshall), 'The Road of the Pilgrim' (Arch Wiggins/Don Osgood) and 'A Prayer for Courage' (Eric Ball) was both as exciting and as musically fulfilling as any singing experience I have had before or since.

In a rehearsal not long after we arrived in Bedlington I remember sitting just 'lapping up' the sounds, chords and textures created by this great Songster Brigade singing James Curnow's 'Christ's Part' and realising – perhaps for the first time (?) – that Christ could, indeed, speak to one's very soul through the ministry of Salvation Army music.

I sat 3rd euphonium in the senior band with Stan Wearmouth and his son David to my left but I began to be featured by the band as a euphonium soloist almost straight away. My favourite solos with band accompaniment, in those days, were Ray Steadman-Allen's 'The Ransomed Host' and Erik Leidzen's 'Home on the Range' (which had now been published in the Festival Series). I tended to keep away from playing the same solos with band accompaniment as I did with piano; as a result I think in all my years as soloist I have only ever played 'The Song Of The Brother' with band accompaniment once yet, with piano, the tally must be several hundred times for the same Leidzen classic solo!

I've mentioned he surname 'Wearmouth' several times already – and that was one of the families that had/have been long-associated with Bedlington Corps. Stan and Jim were two of 7 brothers – they plus Joe and Norman were all in the band and two of them also had sons in the band. Other notable families in the corps were the Hogg, Dixon, Burns and Lightley families. Many of these could trace their roots back to the very earliest days of the corps history and I'm delighted to say that most of them are still represented in the Bedlington Corps today, over forty years since 'our time' there!

But it seemed to me that, even if family played a very large part in Bedlington SA life, the whole corps was like one big family. Sadly, in the years since, I have experienced times where the links between senior and YP corps, or Band and Songsters within a corps have been less than ideal, where some corps folk would have little or no knowledge of what happened in the Home League or Over 60s Club etc. Yet, here I was part of a corps that very much existed as the Body of Christ – with each part deserving of and receiving equal importance, love and care. Each section existed not in any way for its own 'glory' or praise but as a vital part of a thriving corps that was both growing in size and giving so very much back to the community in which it served – and, in doing so, bringing more people, young and old into the knowledge of the saving power of Jesus.

Of course, Bedlington Corps in 1980 was not the 'perfect church' – such a thing doesn't nor ever can exist – but it made a much better effort at trying to be the best it could be than many others, and I truly thank God that he placed me there to be part of it for a while. So much that was life-changing for me and which would go on to shape my own Christian service and ideals came about as a result of my spending time at Bedlington Corps and I treasure all it means to me in my heart right up to today.

Chapter Twenty-Six – Jim, Bands and Healing Hands

Bedlington SA Band, as I have said, was big and could also be loud – very loud, in fact – but BM Jim Burn kept them in control most of the time and could also bring out of the band a beautiful, Spiritual sound that could move a congregation to tears. As for Jim himself, the sight of him conducting the band with tears flowing copiously from his own eyes was one I became quickly accustomed to and loved very much. Jim, like several others in the corps, had been a miner earlier in life but had retrained afterwards to become one of the very best osteopaths in the country. His hands, more than any I've ever met since were truly 'healing hands'. Although the SA rarely ventures into a healing ministry in the way that, say, a Pentecostal church might*, I am 100% certain that all the healing power of the Holy Spirit was spread far and wide through Jim Burn's ministry.

(This was not always the case, by the way – a study of the 'earliest days' of the army shows us that such a ministry did take place – the great songwriter Col. William Pearson – writer of 'Joy in the Salvation Army' was just one early officer blessed with the Spiritual gift of healing and he often used it in SA meetings.)

Of all the people I have ever met Jesus shone through Jim Burn in a way I have hardly ever experienced. He was gentle, kind, patient, encouraging and I loved him so dearly – so, what a thrill it was for me when we moved to live next door to him!

I have mentioned in this book previously how my dad seemed to be sent to corps where, very often, something needed to be done about property – and Bedlington upheld this 'tradition' – for, not long after he was appointed to the corps, the decision was made to move the 'Quarters' from the council estate – the corps deciding to buy a house rather than renting. After viewing several houses it was decided to buy 2 High Ridge, a most beautiful house just around the corner from the hall – only The Red Lion pub and a roundabout lay between them, if I remember correctly!

By this time I was the band's solo euphonium player, Stan having taken some time out of his own ministry just then. He, and his son David (who now formed, with me, what must have been one of the youngest euphonium sections in the SA) lived just a few doors further along. David – who is only 6 months or so older than me - bred budgies for a hobby and we could hear his menagerie clearly from our own (concrete again) back garden!

As usual...I digress...we used to see from our front window Jim Burns' patients arrive for their treatment. Old men, doubled up with pain would walk into his house with sticks and would emerge an hour later walking straight and stick-less! It was amazing! Famous footballers would also arrive there – one example being the late Kevin Beattie whose career had been plagued by knee problems – but he kept his career going much longer with the help of Jim's 'touch'. My own dad was a recipient of the BM's expertise as, later on I was myself. Dad had suffered sciatica ever since he had felt a 'twinge' in his back over twenty years earlier while collecting on a flag day at Newcastle City Temple while he was a Youth Officer. Dad was telling Jim one day about the 'numbness' he often felt in his leg – so Jim told him to get onto his couch and he soon discovered that 5 of dad's inter-vertebral discs had become displaced over time. With his thumbs he manipulated each back into place and dad returned home without 'pins and needles' in his feet for the first time he could remember!

My own 'accident' occurred while helping my dad to park in a small space on a piece of waste land near St James' Park before a football match. As dad reversed into the space I stood behind his purple Ford Cortina waving him on, and then saying 'stop' when he was close enough. Of course, dad being quite seriously deaf didn't hear me say it…or even when I shouted it! Only when I screamed with my knee firmly wedged between two car bumpers did he stop – and by then, it later transpired, the cartilages in my left knee had found themselves a new home in and around my patella rather than behind it! Jim sat me down, got me to bend my knee and lift my ankle off the ground, moved his hand around my knee and then, with a click of his thumb pressed the offending cartilages back to where they ought to have been! I had to call in his house after school every day for several months to have them put back until, eventually, they stayed in! Inevitably, they started coming out again as soon as I rebegan riding my bike but back we went and things were a lot better in time!

Dad and I, however, were not the only members of our family Jim helped. When my mum's sister and her family came to stay with us

Jim managed to find out that my cousin was unable to do any PE at school due to bad knees – this being a result of a fall from a wall many years before when she was a very small child. His investigations discovered that she had dislocated both knees and this had never been properly treated.

The problem was, of course, that correcting such a problem – one that had existed for years – would normally have taken a lengthy course of treatment, but the family lived many miles away on the South Coast. Jim said he 'could' do it all at once but that the pain would be almost unbearable – my cousin WOULD be sick, he warned. Yet brave Denise wanted so much to be able to do what other children did and so she asked for the treatment. Yes, she was sick, of course – but within months she was in the school netball team and now, some forty years later, she has started running 10km road races! Healing hands? Oh yes! Yes, Lord, indeed!

Bedlington Band, under BM Jim's baton may not have had the finesse of some of the wider Army's 'great' bands like Enfield or Chalk Farm but they played with a passion I have never seen or heard matched. They could, and did, make beautiful music and the wonderful tone of Dennis Todd on top cornet made sharing special moments between he and myself in pieces such as 'The Light Of The World' and 'The Challenge of the Cross' (both by Dean Goffin) precious experiences from my musical memories.

We did away weekends at various places including Leith (Edinburgh) where a former Bedlington Bandsman, Ted Turnbull, had relocated through work and Leeds West Hunslet but most of our playing was done locally in churches and nearby corps. The band was even 'privileged' to be the only one ever allowed to march on the Great North Road (the A1) which we did in November each year as part of the Remembrance events. We held open-air meetings at least once every Sunday as far away as Ashington (which had no SA corps itself in those days) and were delighted one day when a white-haired, older man came down to greet the band – I was told that he was Jackie Milburn, one of Newcastle United's greatest ever footballers and a true 'legend'! My dad had spoken of him in reverent tones for as long as I could remember!

I fondly remember many of the bandsmen from those days with their own influence and interaction with my life:

- Norman Dixon on soprano cornet who loved cricket as much as I did and could chat about great names and matches from the past. Norman's son Brian was the singing company leader, a fine trombone player and an exceptional vocal soloist. I have always loved singing Joy Webb's 'There Will Be God' but I hold Brian's version of that solo as an exemplar to this day. Brian was also the captain of Bedlington Cricket Club, a very good opening batsman, and I spent a lot of time at the club myself playing for the Colts team. Sadly, Norman was Promoted to Glory during our time in Bedlington after developing cancer but his infectious passion for God, his strong voice and distinctive soprano 'vibrato' will always stay with me. Brian, his wife and their twin daughters – then just babies – are still part of the corps today.

- Syd Tweddle – the Torchbearer/Youth Club Leader (also the father of twin daughters) played flugel horn, and like Norman Dixon and BM Burn was part of the famed Bedlington Male Voice Party.

- CS Gordon Lightley – he played front row cornet and was corps pianist when pieces needed to be played 'by ear' – i.e. there was no music or just the melody line from the old chorus book. Gordon was also a strong singer and a lovely Christian man – his three sons Keith (YPSM), Colin and Ian were also in the band when we first came to the corps although Ian left a short time later. Keith was Wicket Keeper in the same Bedlington cricket team that Brian captained. Gordon's Christmas card was always the first I received each year for the rest of his life and I was glad to have tea with him on a return to the town many years later after he had moved from his house 'Penlan' into a new development nearer the SA hall.

- CT John Laverick was a strong and kind man, a very special friend to my family (especially my sister Eira).

- Ken Hogg was Recruiting Sergeant, top trombone and another wonderful man of God I was privileged to know. His father Stephen was still in the corps back then as was his son Glen, an excellent cornet player and one of my best friends in the Corps.

- Walter Doyle, who played baritone seemed old to me even then – yet he lived for many more years and remained active and just as positive an influence on all he met. When I went back to the corps with my mum to lead a weekend I stayed with him and his wife Dora. Walter's sons Colin and Brian both played tenor horn in the band at that time and both sons married while we were at the corps.

- George Nichol was Corps/Songster Pianist and the band's bass trombone player. His three sons Desmond and twins John and Ian were also in the band. George accompanied me on many occasions when I was asked to be a euphonium soloist and also remained a good friend for the rest of his life.

I also played with the very large YP Band at Bedlington at first. They were led by John Robertson who played Eb bass in the senior band. The music they used was mostly from the Triumph Series but not just the simpler choices – we played the bigger suites and selections like 'Joy and Devotion' by Howard Davies as well as marches like 'God's Children (William Himes). Of particular interest was the new Leslie

Condon Suite in 1981 called 'Blyth Heritage'. Blyth is a seaside town less than five miles from Bedlington but its place in Salvation Army history is far greater than Bedlington's own – for John Roberts began all children's ministry in The Salvation Army right there back in 1880. We even took part in special celebrations in the old Army hall in Blyth to mark the centenary of this work, for which a musical was written by Keith Banks – 'John Roberts Celebration Party'. Sadly, SA work in Blyth ended some years ago and the hall is now used as a mosque.

Brian Dixon, as I mentioned earlier, was a very enthusiastic Singing Company Leader and, although I was not in the group at that time I followed their progress closely as my two younger sisters Eira and Ruth were keen participants. The YP Band and Singing Company often travelled together to perform musical festivals and have 'away weekends' at SA centres including Doncaster and Scarborough.

I have written several times by now about how much dad loved the children in the various corps where he served as CO. Bedlington was no different and he just loved to get on the children's 'level' and enjoy a bit of fun and banter with them. One Christmas morning he asked, in advance, if each child could bring one of their presents to the meeting. Young Philip Burn, son of songster leader Eric, lined up on the platform wearing the bright red boxing gloves Santa had, obviously, brought him that morning. Dad pretended not to know what they were and bent down low to the young lad's side and asked, "What do you do with those then?" expecting Philip to bop him gently on the cheek. The boy wound back his arm and caught dad's chin with a right hook that

would have pleased Henry Cooper…dad was more wary after that!
Philip has worked for the Salvation Army in Texas for almost all his
adult life.

Another special little girl in the YP corps was Joanne Greenacre.
Joanne was born with spina biffida and, although she could walk a little
with callipers and crutches at the time she has spent the majority of her
life in a wheelchair. I can remember being so moved by her regular
singing of the children's song 'If I Were a Butterfly' and, in the chorus,
'Mr Noah Built an Ark' she would jump as best she could when doing
the actions for 'kangaroo'. She turned seven during our stay at
Bedlington and was asked if she wanted to become a Junior Soldier.
Asking what she had to do she was told that she had to 'give her heart to
Jesus'. "Oh no," she replied – "I've had enough operations!" I know
dad was as proud to enrol her as he ever was to enrol anyone and Joanne
is still part of the corps today.

Three more pictures from Bedlington – Joanne's enrolment as a Junior Soldier and a press clipping from the local newspaper marking a sponsored walk completed by the band to raise money for new instruments. Finally mum with some local officers (BM Jim Burn, left Brenda Nichol and RS Ken Hoff right) at a Sunbury Court event.

Blow me down!

A heavenly surprise for Army marchers

• THEY'RE HERE: Two young members of the band arrive back at the centre cheered by well-wishers with the instruments.

ONWARD Christian soldiers — the Army has been on the march to bring in brass for the band.

A dozen members of Bedlington Salvation Army Corps have just taken part in a 30-mile sponsored walk to raise cash for new instruments.

But blow me — when the bandsmen arrived back home all puffed out after the hike there was a stock of new instruments ready for them.

"The sponsored walk was just one of the many things that we have been doing to raise money for new instruments over the last three years. The walkers were really cheered to find new instruments waiting for them when they came back from the walk," said Major Kenneth Harry, commanding officer of the Bedlington Salvation Army Corps.

"When I arrived here three years ago it was obvious that our band needed new instruments."

NEWS DIGEST

Man falls to death

A Gateshead man plunged to his death from the upper storey of a block of flats...

Chapter Twenty-Seven – Away from the Army...

I quite often wonder how we had time for anything else besides Salvation Army activities while at Bedlington – but we did, and lots of it! Of course, I was in the 6th Form at school, having duly received my full set of 'O Level' passes. Like I said earlier, I HAD thought school was behind me after Stoke-On-Trent but there was no '6th Form College' system in place in Northumberland in 1979 and so I found myself enrolled in a very historic educational establishment, King Edward VI School, in nearby Morpeth. Getting there and back meant two 25 minute bus journeys each day and...dread of all dreads...I had to go back into school uniform for the first time in years...yes, I KNOW I said so already, but ...really!. All this did my self-esteem no good at all – I felt like I was being forced to be a little kid again, to be honest and my dislike of the school, its uniform and the other things were, I think, to blame for my not showing much interest at all in my academic progress for the two years I spent at the school. Having loved school so much for the whole of my time as a pupil until then I must confess to 'switching off' in Morpeth, I'm afraid.

In retrospect, I also chose very much the wrong subjects for me there. I can remember sitting in a Biology lesson at Stanfield High School back in Burslem and hearing my teacher Mr. Pemberton tell the class that dentists earned a lot of money – at the time I'm sure he said around £12,000 a year. From that moment something lit a light bulb in my head, the pound signs flashed before my eyes and I decided that all I wanted to be when I grew up was to become a dentist...

The fact I wasn't remotely interested in dentistry, have always had a phobia of seeing people without their teeth in and hate second-hand breath seemed like total irrelevances…I was going to be a dentist! And so I chose to study Physics, Chemistry and Biology at A Level.

Had I chosen English, Music and History my whole life might have been very different…but I didn't: Chem, Phys and Biol it was – and I sank without trace. I loved doing the Chemistry experiments and fancied my gorgeous Chemistry teacher Miss Russell (who was only about 5 years older than us students) something rotten – and that, at least, kept me trying a bit in that subject. (Whether trying to do well or whether I was trying to impress Miss Russell made no difference! Eventually she married, became Mrs. Oaten and moved away to Winchester, anyway!)

Physics went right over my head from day one. I'm sure that the two teachers we had for that subject were excellent scientists and teachers but I had no idea what I was doing there besides the futile chase for grades that might lead to dentistry college. That was never going to be enough to overcome the Everest I was facing. I should have asked for help but I never did. I hid my problems from my parents with teenage bravado and my natural 'acting skills' as I gurgled and went under. By the Upper Sixth I was sneaking off to practice rooms to play the piano during Physics lessons or even, I'm ashamed to admit, bunking off to town with my pal, Colin Nicholson, to play snooker at the YMCA. If my dad had known this I'd have soon discovered that I wasn't too old to face his wrath quite yet!

In December 1980 I was woken one Tuesday morning by my mum knocking on my bedroom door. Just a couple of weeks earlier I had queued at the record shop in Eldon Square, Newcastle to buy the first LP released by my hero John Lennon in over five years. That morning, my headphones were on the floor beside my bed and the LP sleeve of 'Double Fantasy' was on top of the Music Centre next to me where I had listened to it yet again before going to sleep the night before.

"Prepare yourself for a shock," mum said. I thought, immediately, that one of my grandparents must have died. If they HAD done so it would have been far less of a shock than when she told me it was John Lennon that had been shot!

"How is he?" I asked her but she shook her head sadly to let me know he had died. It was completely unbelievable! That just couldn't be true. I sat on the floor with my old 'twiddle top' radio set and desperately searched for any station that WASN'T playing 'Imagine' or some Beatles song – a station where SOMEONE would tell me what I wanted to hear – that my mum was WRONG. Alas, of course, that could not be. My hero John Lennon – John from The Beatles – had been killed in New York outside the apartment buildings where he had lived. The last song I had heard the night before on Side One was 'Beautiful Boy' – a gorgeous lullaby to John's five year old son, Sean. My thoughts turned to Sean – now fatherless as John himself had been yet for a very different reason.

A year or so earlier, as mentioned briefly above, dad had brought two Vox electric guitars home from DHQ where they had been donated for youth work somewhere in the Northern Division. I had taken one and started to teach myself guitar. My mum taught me my first few chords (as she had done many years before for Joy Webb who later formed The Salvation Army's own chart-bound beat group 'The Joy Strings)'. Then I bought a chord book and worked my way through 'The Beatles Complete' with its help. Before heading for school somewhat late that Tuesday morning I hung the guitar up in my bedroom window and surrounded it with Beatles pictures and LP covers – my John Lennon 'shrine' I suppose – and, when I got back home still rather dazed and upset, there were several cards and letters through our letter box thanking me for the display and sharing my teenage grief.

Colin and I asked the head teacher at school if we could mark John's death by playing his music during 'General Studies' the next day. All the sixth form had General Studies on Wednesday afternoons and they could choose music, sport or do homework – whatever was 'on the programme'. He replied by telling us we could indeed play John Lennon music – on the condition that for every record we played we performed two songs live ourselves, either on piano or guitar, singing or instrumental! We thought to ourselves, OK, let's do it, there'll only be a couple of people turn up. Even in 1980 The Beatles weren't as popular as they had been 15 years earlier, after all.

So, we booked the Music Room and added the 'event' to the General Studies list for the next day. We set up the room for our concert and were rather surprised when quite a few people started turning up. Then more…and more! Soon we realised the music room was not going to be big enough so we moved into the nearby school hall and Colin and I played our way through songs and records for the next couple of hours or so while rows and rows of weeping girls (some wearing Beatles scarves and round John Lennon spectacles) lapped up every note and clapped at the end of the songs. That was a surreal experience then and it still seems surreal recalling it today some 45 years later!

Although music seemed to dominate most areas of my life at that time there were a few other activities that also managed to find a way into my busy lifestyle – and, as I mentioned earlier, one of them was cricket. I mentioned how I played for Bedlington Colts team, but I had limited success as a player. I won a match against local rivals Bomarsund CC, coming in with 9 balls remaining and getting the 27 we had needed to win but, pushed up to opening the bat after that, a couple of ducks put me back in my place. Despite wanting to, I never got the chance to bowl for the team and then something else took over…

My dad had been a football referee for many years, as I've mentioned before and, once his refereeing days were over, he had taken up cricket umpiring while in Camborne then in Torquay and Stoke. Moving to Northumberland we discovered there were two different leagues – to me they were the 'red one' and the 'yellow one' (because those were the colours of the two yearbooks) or the 'posh' one and the 'other' one (because the 'red one' thought itself much bigger and more important than the 'yellow one'.) Bedlington were in the 'yellow' league whereas the 'red league' was home to the top teams like Benwell, Ashington and County Club who played at Jesmond in Newcastle, the home of Northumberland County Cricket Club. The 'red league' could afford each side to have a 'professional' player who was usually an ex county or a test match player at the end of his career. At the time we were there these pros included Pakistani legend Mushtaq Mohammed, Indian spinner Dilip Doshi and ex-Kent and England fast bowler Norman Graham.

Since the Camborne days I had usually gone with my father when he umpired matches unless it was either still the football season and I had my season ticket to a game at Stoke City's old Victoria Ground or St James' Park or on the rare occasion I was playing cricket myself. One day dad turned up at Benwell Hill CC in Newcastle and his fellow umpire failed to arrive for the match. Usually, on such occasions, one of the batting side would come out and stand at square leg while the officiating umpire stood at the stumps at both ends to manage the 'action'. On this occasion, however, unbeknownst to me, dad offered my services in the dressing room,

"Marc knows the Laws of the Game back to front!" he assured them and, so, I found myself not only standing in the game but, by all accounts, doing quite well. The amount of cricket I had watched each summer had stood me in good stead. After each game the league's expectation was that the two captains would 'mark' the umpires and send the marks to the league secretary. My marks were obviously good enough that, a few days later I had a phone call from the secretary offering me a place on the umpires panel and my own umpiring fixtures for the rest of the season. That's how I instantly became a cricket umpire with £10 a match (plus travelling expenses) standing in games with Test Cricketers playing. What an amazing childhood I had! Just a few games later dad and I were put down to officiate a match together – with me listed as the 'senior umpire'. You can, perhaps, imagine how that went down I'm sure!

I was 'senior umpire' one day when County Club were the visitors in Benwell. I always got on well with the Benwell team, especially their captain, a local GP who originated from Pakistan. Benwell batted first on a cloudy, rather dull day and former Kent bowler Norman Graham (left), all 6 feet 8 inches of him and now aged 38 bowled the whole innings from my end. That was 25 overs that he bowled his overs very..........very..........slowly! We usually had the between-innings tea (a marvellous spread prepared by the players' wives with sandwiches, cakes and much more) around 4pm but, by the time Graham completed his marathon effort we ate at 5. As a consequence, by the 30 over mark in County Club's reply it was getting quite dark. 5 overs later I called the game off when a ball lost after a boundary had been hit turned out to be nearly 100 yards away from where the fielder had been looking. It really was deep into twilight. Norman Graham was livid – he tried to approach me as I left the pitch but I managed to avoid him as I made it back to the safety of the umpire's changing room. The only problem was I hadn't yet received my umpire's fee or expenses so I needed to go back into the bar to collect it. Graham was there, larger than ever! He approached me and shook my hand.

"You were completely right," he said, "and very brave for such a young man." Then he smiled and added, "but I still hate you!"

In the winter, for dad and I, it was always football and wherever we were we watched and supported the local team. We saw Newport County together, watched Huddersfield Town's only season in the top division for decades in 1971, Torquay United's bottom tier struggles, Stoke City AND Port Vale on alternate Saturdays (as dad had done in Liverpool during his Youth Officer days with Liverpool and Everton) and now we watched Newcastle United, standing each week on the famous Gallowgate but watching one of the poorest sides the club had had for many years. If we had been just a couple of years later Keegan and Beardsley would have been on the scene and much better times were ahead for the 'Toon' but the best we witnessed during our time was the breakthrough of a young lad who had previously worked in a sausage factory in Tow Law- the young Chris Waddle. I still keep an eye out for all these teams' results but, like dad, it was always Cardiff City we really 'supported' from afar although this also changed in dad's retirement when we watched Portsmouth FC together for many years. I have also been a Liverpool supporter from the day they signed my hero 'Tosh' (John Toshack) from Cardiff.

One way or another, though, music was taking a bigger and bigger role in my life already by the time I reached 6th form. I sang with an excellent school choir at 'King Eds' under Mr Doswell's direction and also played with a good school orchestra (not as good as the one in Stoke but close). The orchestra was led by the school's second music teacher Mrs (Olga) South – and it didn't take me long to discover that she used to be a Salvationist and had been a member of the prestigious 'National Songsters' in the 1960s under the direction of Muriel Packham. Through my participation in the school orchestra I was also appointed principal trombone for the Northumberland Schools Orchestra – something that stands out as a beacon of enjoyment in what was a thoroughly depressing and hated two years in my educational life.

The NSO met for rehearsals occasionally throughout the year but, mainly, got together for a week at a time at the Police Training School in Ponteland, near Newcastle. There, we learned and rehearsed the repertoire for our big, annual concert. The orchestra was conducted by Ian Reid, a Scottish musician who worked in London with one of the opera houses. Amongst the pieces we played were Tchaikovsky's 5th Symphony and Malcolm Arnold's great, fun piece 'Tam O'Shanter' – much loved by me, of course, because it featured a trombone solo in which I had to play as if I were drunk and with glissandi all over the place! Wonderful! I made some good friends in that orchestra, some of whom I am still in touch with today through Facebook.

I mentioned my friend Colin Nicholson earlier. He was a superb piano student – a far better pianist even then that I ever would be – but we loved to play and improvise duets together. Amongst the 'proper' pieces we rehearsed and enjoyed playing were 'Popular Song' from the 'Façade' Suite by William Walton and Ravel's 'Dolly Suite' but much more popular with our friends was our 'magnum opus': 'Concerto in TV Major'. This was a lengthy piece we improvised together based on popular TV themes and adverts of the day. Starting with children's TV we had the themes from 'Paddington' and 'The Mr Men' before the 'News' interrupted and adult programmes started including 'Last of the Summer Wine', 'Mastermind', 'Crossroads' AND 'Coronation Street' (ending with the two being played at the same time as our imaginary viewers battled for control of the TV set). Then we had some adverts ('a finger of fudge is just enough to give your kids a treat' and 'we are the lads from country life and you can't put a better bit'o' butter on your knife') . Then the piece ended with a few more tunes and a big 'concerto' finale in which bits of all the featured tunes came together in a televisual cornucopia (or cacophony!).

This particular story should probably come later, maybe even in a different volume, but Colin and I ended up at Music College together in Colchester a few years later and we decided to perform a joint recital there as part of our studies. In the recital we both played some incredibly difficult and rather 'high-brow' pieces. Colin played Chopin's 'Fantaisie-Impromptu' and I included 'Piece en Mi Benol Mineur' by J Guy Ropartz and the Horovitz Euphonium Concerto. It's fair to say, that we 'wowed' the assembled audience somewhat…but then, we decided to end our recital by resurrecting our duet concerto – played on 2 wonderful Steinway Grand Pianos. The audience loved it, some of our lecturers appeared to enjoy it a little less – but we both like to think that they enjoyed it somewhat more than they let on!

At school both Colin and I had our piano lessons with a rather splendid old lady called Gladys Willis. Gladys must have been well into her 80s and she lived in a very large house at the bottom of a hill near the school in Morpeth. Gladys had 'made her name' as a renowned BBC accompanist and now lived out her days in the lovely, Northumberland town. She used to enter me for Music Festivals; locally the Wansbeck Music Festival was the main event, and I remember twice entering a piano competition to play Debussy, the first time it was 'La Cathedrale Engloutie' (the submerged cathedral) and the second time around I played 'Minstrels' – but, for me, this was merely 'for the experience' – up against the likes of Colin I never stood a chance of winning…but that was not the case when it came to the brass classes! The Wansbeck Music Festival, incidentally, still awards a trophy each year called the Gladys Willis Memorial Cup in memory and honour of our old piano teacher.

I always say that I have been a self-taught euphonium player. Do you remember I mentioned a story 'way' back in a previous chapter about dad playing me the 78 rpm record of Victor Saywell playing 'The Warrior' and telling me, "When you can play like that, you know you've arrived?" Well, when I first went onto euphonium (see the story in the

Torquay chapters) dad arranged for me to have a few lessons with Ret SL Tout, a very well-respected SA musician. I, of course, asked to learn 'The Warrior', a 1938 SA solo by Phil Catalinet, probably because I wanted to 'arrive' as soon as I could! Now, whether it was the 'artistic license' of Victor Saywell or the necessity to split the solo into two halves for a 78 record, the soloist on the record starts the 'triplet' variation by slightly pausing the first three notes. I had heard this and I liked it…so, when I played it in my lesson, I did the same – and was promptly stopped by SL Tout. He asked me why I had done what I'd done and I replied that I'd simply played it like the record. He told me there was no need to 'pause' the notes and not to do it. I tried it that way but I didn't like it so, the next time, I went back to my pausing.

The kind old man, to whom I swear to you, I bore neither any ill will at all, nor any intent to upset (remember I was just eleven years old at the time), told me to carry on practicing while he left the room. About twenty minutes later my extremely angry dad came in and he told me that he'd found the old man upset in his car outside as I'd been 'very rude' to him and refused to do as I was told. That was the end of my euphonium lessons – completely – until I reached music college! I had learned the 'basics' of playing from Ron Taylor at Knottingley and George Brooke at Heckmondwike but, since then all I had 'learned' about brass playing I had learned 'on the job' playing with a band or on my own in hours and hours of practice on my own. I still feel very guilty that I inadvertently upset that lovely man but I hope that, in my own teaching later in life, I have tried to be a little more patient and understanding.

At school in Stoke I went to play each week to a peripatetic brass teacher – I think his name was Wilson Hawkins – but he was a bass trombonist who admitted he had nothing to offer a euphoniumist like me and we often just sat and chatted about music or bands. He did enter me for my Grade VIII euphonium in 1978 when I was just 15 and which I passed with distinction dropping only 7 marks. He never called himself my teacher although he undoubtedly honed my performances of those exam pieces and I'm grateful to him not just for that – but, mainly, for getting me out of an hour of Maths every week!

In the Wansbeck Music Festival of 1981, it would seem that I excelled myself somewhat, according to the following newspaper article anyway! Please excuse the dreadful jacket and the worst attempt EVER at a Beatles haircut in the photograph!

I won the Open Brass competition playing 'La Belle Americaine' (John Hartmann) accompanied by George Nichol from the army and was awarded the highest mark in the whole competition (94/100) to win the Dussart Trophy.

In addition, I had been in the piano competition (see above), and I had not just accompanied Eira in the singing and woodwind contests but had actually composed the pieces she played in them. So, they saw fit to feature me in the local newspaper along with my trophy and my sister with her oboe. Fame at last!

MUSICAL MARC

EIGHTEEN - YEAR - OLD Marc Harry played the euphonium so well in Wansbeck Music Festival that he walked off with the competition's highest mark.

And he was also the writer of a song and composer of an oboe sonata which his sister performed.

Marc, of High Ridge, Bedlington, a pupil at the King Edward VI School in Morpeth won the Dussart Trophy, the first time it has been awarded, with 94 marks for his outstanding performance in the open solo brass instrument class.

He also played in the open piano solo and, although he did not win, judges praised the exceptional standard of all competitors.

Marc started his musical career in the Salvation Army when he was about six. His father is Major Ken Harry, of Bedlington SA.

CONCERTO

"I wrote the oboe sonata when I was 16, and Eira played the first movement" said Marc, "She also sang a song called Beautiful World, but neither of them won."

He has also written a euphonium concerto, but there's a snag.

"I haven't played it yet because I can't find a piano accompanist. Everyone says it's too hard. But I have a friend at school who may have a try.

Marc has composed several pieces for the Salvation Army — chorales, marches and up-tempo songs — and he also finds time to give piano lessons to 10 pupils.

Recently Marc gave a general studies lecture at school about his music and Eira, also a pupil at King Edward, and friend Colin Nicholson played some of his compositions.

Last year he entered the Royal College of Music Associated Board Scholarship competition for students who had gained distinctions in grade eight examinations.

Marc was selected for the last 13 out of 200 entrants but just failed to win a scholarship.

And three years ago he won a trophy as the best promising musician at a course at the Salvation Army Junior National Music School.

He also plays trombone with the Northumberland School Orchestra.

But when he leaves school, after A levels this summer his intentions aren't too musical. He hopes to train to be a dentist.

Music festival results on Page Three.

Marc Harry and his sister, Eira.

The lack of a euphonium teacher DID cause me a problem on one occasion, I must admit: I was entered into the BBC Young Musician of the Year Competition and travelled to York for one of the rounds of the competition. What a good teacher would have done for me on that occasion would have been to help me to assemble a varied programme that would both impress the judges and also have enough variety to fulfil the requirements of the competition. That was something I had, realistically, no chance of doing by myself. And so I played two Air Varie solos on the day, both of which scored very high marks. A simple slow melody and, maybe a little classical transcription or study would have seen me progress but, as the judges explained to me in person later (very apologetically, in fact) they had had to 'disqualify me' for essentially playing two 'almost identical' pieces of music and, therefore, having my overall mark for them divided by two. I lived and learned, though it was, of course, a big disappointment at the time!

There are two more stories from my Bedlington years that concerned musical compositions that I feel I ought to share. The famed song 'My Way' by Paul Anka and made famous by Frank Sinatra contains a line we all know: 'Regrets? I've had a few," and one of the only regrets I have in my Salvation Army life is that I am not, and I doubt I ever will be a published composer of SA music. As I wrote earlier I have written 315 songs to date, entire musicals, band pieces and lots more – songs that were used to great effect dutring my later years with the 'Blood and Fire' rock band and in my own solo ministry all round the army world. Yet there are none in SA publications at all. That is MY FAULT, and no-one else's. Pride and stupidity are very often unnecessary obstacles to God's work and my regret is that I allowed them to get in the way as I did.

I entered a competition in the Northern Division to compose a song to words by Army songwriter Bram Back. The beautiful words, titled 'Love Alone' were distributed to all who entered the 'music writing' competition and a tune 'Durrington' by Maurice Ozanne was given to those who wanted to write lyrics. Eira and I decided to enter the competition but, to avoid competing against each other, I entered the music contest and Eira the lyrics. The prize was to be presented by the British Commissioner (Territorial Commander in modern parlance) John Needham at a Divisional celebration meeting and the winning entries submitted to the SA Music Council for future publication.

Eira and I both won! We received the congratulations of the Commissioner *(see picture below)* and the song 'Love Alone' became an instant 'hit', much loved whenever I , or my mum and dad as a duet, sang it in meetings. However, In the 44 years since this success 'Love Alone' has still not been published by the SA (as promised) for wider use. This was a disappointment then, as it still is today.

In addition, our Divisional Youth Secretary, Major Cliff Hurcombe, gave me a wonderful opportunity that was both exciting and a challenge. The united Corps Cadets of the division had been asked to produce the epilogue for the National Corps Cadet Rally at the Royal Albert Hall that year. The theme chosen for the event was 'You're only Young Once' – recognising the temptations young people faced in an ever more secular world, with the intention of this leading into the prayer session at the conclusion of the rally and, hopefully, many young people kneeling in rededication.

I duly wrote two songs, 'You're Only Young Once' a rock and roll number with dance routine to match, followed by 'Consecration', the words of which read,

I consecrate my life to You,

I've taken up my cross

To follow You where'ere You lead,

My Lord.

My life, my all I give to You,

Accept my offering, Lord

And use my life to do Your will,

I pray.

Rehearsing with the other youngsters I realised what a blessing these words were – I've never found writing lyrics easy but these seemed to come so naturally I could hardly claim authorship. I prayed daily that the epilogue might have the desired effect at the Corps Cadet rally and that other young people's lives might be changed. But, one day at home in the SA Quarters (officer's home) my dad passed me the telephone. On the other end of the line was Colonel John Larsson, the National Youth Secretary to tell me personally that my songs would not be used at all.

His claim that the first song was 'too catchy' didn't quite convince me that youngsters might go away from the event singing 'You're only young once so you have to live it up' rather than the intended message. I argued (politely) with the Colonel (later General) that his own song 'Damascus' (from 'Spirit!') had many similarities but he responded that one song from a two hour musical held less importance than one from a two song epilogue...nothing he said could shield me from the shattering disappointment his message conveyed. I have no idea what substitute item Major Hurcombe managed to assemble in the time remaining because I never attended the rally – and I never sent another piece of music to the army to be considered for publication. I KNOW 100% that I was wrong and should have overcome my hurt – hence why I began this section of the book with 'regrets'.

The Summer of 1981 arrived and, with it, the inevitable arrival at 2 High Ridge of my A Level results. Because of my almost complete avoidance of my Physics course at school I had failed to achieve the 'Three Cs' I had needed to secure the place on the BDS course at Manchester University that I had been provisionally offered. And so ended my career as a dentist – along with my realistic chances of being as rich as I might have hoped later in life!

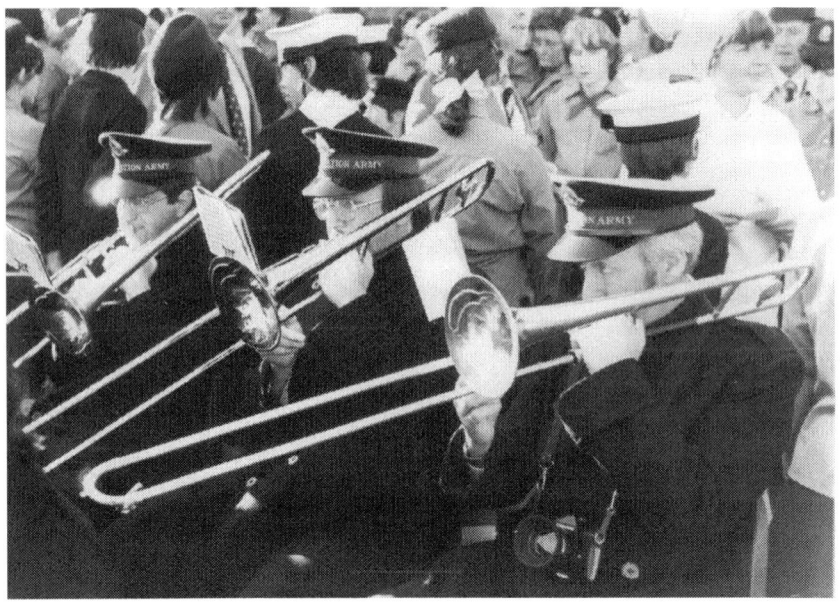

About half the trombone section in Bedlington Band – Ken Hogg, Brian Dixon and Colin Lightley. Ken, (the corps Recruiting Sergeant) built a full-size boat in his back garden!

I'm pretty certain my parents were far more worried about my failure to get into university than I was at the time. I admit I had absolutely no idea what I was going to do after August 1981 or what I even wanted to do at that time – like Dickens's Mr Micawber in 'David Copperfield' I thought 'something will come up'. Of course, it did.

We had all gone to bed after a busy Sunday at the corps at the beginning of September when my bedroom door almost burst open. Dad, in his striped pyjamas, stood beside my bed waving an advertisement he'd found in his Sunday newspaper. Somewhere called the Colchester Institute was offering students the chance to enrol for a BA (honours) degree course in Music if they had 2 A Levels. I had 2 but also had the musical equivalent in Grade VIII practical and theory.

The next morning dad rang the Vice Principal who happened to be BM Michael Clack of Chalk Farm (conducting, opposite) and, as I wrote in an earlier chapter, a close family friend.

Within a couple of days I was in Essex auditioning for a course that had already begun – and a few days after that I was dropped at a house in Colchester in which I had, with the help of the Institute's Christian Union rented a room to sleep in. I arrived with my clothes, records and record player, my instruments and with a place on the BA (hons) Music course duly offered and accepted.

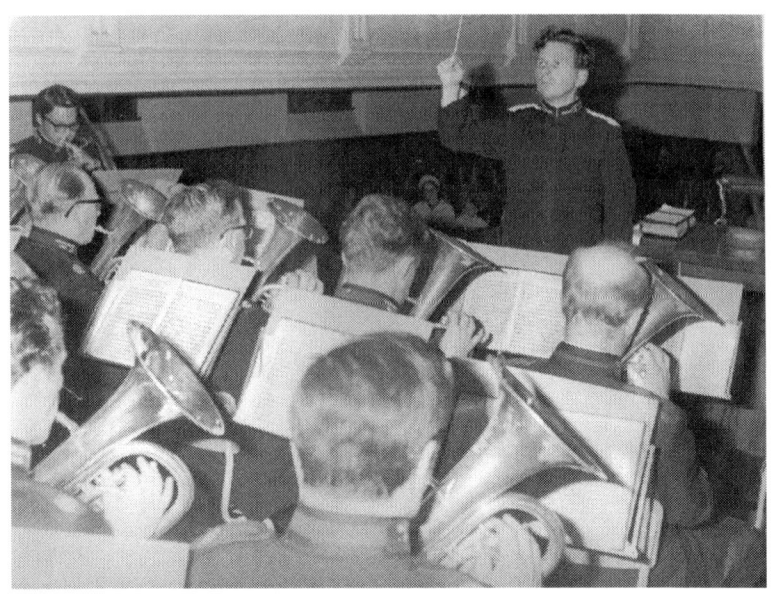

It seemed a whirlwind back then and the memory is no less hectic now…but I had 'left home' and the immediate experience of being an 'OK' was over, for three years at least.

So, mum and dad, Eira and Ruth were left behind in Bedlington and I moved to Essex. When I turned up at the corps in Colchester that weekend I was, for the very first time in my life, NOT the 'Officer's Kid' – and so much happened to me during those three years I'd need another book – let alone telling how God has continued to bless and use me in the subsequent 44 years!

So…how to end this collection of extraordinary stories? In 1982 the family moved down to Felixstowe, Suffolk. Two years later their move to Portsmouth Citadel coincided with me finishing my degree course – so I moved with them to the south coast – and I was to then live in that City for the next 31 years, firstly with them (I was an OK again!) and, subsequently, in my own house after marrying in 1987 and having my own 3 sons born in the city. Major & Mrs Harry had three further appointments in their Salvation Army officership: Southampton Shirley (1987-90), Wrexham, where I'd been born all those years ago (1990-92) and Dudley (1992-93).

Sadly, at the last of these appointments my father suffered a stroke while taking part in the Annual Appeal. This necessitated an early retirement (he was 63) for he and mum (although mum was only 53 – these days she would have had to carry on working as a single, married officer!)

They retired, firstly, to Caversham, near Reading but dad's health continued to decline. In 1995 he lost a leg to diabetes and, with the Caversham house having steps from both front and back doors, the Salvation Army graciously allowed them a move down to the Portsmouth area, where Ruth and I lived. They chose their own beautiful bungalow and, moving in 1996, they shared 6 happy years there until dad's Promotion to Glory in April 2002.

Sadly, my marriage came to an end in 2005 and the 2 older boys stayed with me. Our youngest son, Ieuan, we shared for half a week each until my ex-wife moved away from the area and Ieuan stayed with his brothers in Portsmouth during the week, spending weekends with his mum in Worthing. My mum moved up to Lincoln so she could be nearer my other sister Eira – moving, in December 2010, to a lovely bungalow where she remained very happily until moving into a care home a year before her Promotion to Glory in November 2022.

I served in The Salvation Army at Portsmouth Citadel for many years as solo euphonium in the band, playing solos in places as varied as Belgium and the USA. I sang as soloist on several of the very popular CD recordings made by Portsmouth Citadel Songsters and also added glockenspiel, euphonium and keyboard to others before, finally, serving as pianist with that wonderful Brigade under the superb eadership of John Bird. They were, largely, very happy and fulfilling years of service!

I, having had to sell the family home after the separation and the subsequent deterioration of my own health, moved with the boys into various rented houses for the next 8 years – these were difficult years in so many ways as I tried my best to help Morgan, Lewis and Ieuan to grow in stature and wisdom...They were mostly, quite unhappy years for me personally and, sadly, I could see no better future ahead. Everything was to change, though, in 2014 – and a whole 'new life' began...but that's another story.*

*(In brief, I met a young lady from Lincoln SA who had been tragically widowed at the young age of 33. We married in September 2015 and now have two beautiful daughters Emily Grace and Bronwyn Gwen – the latter born on my birthday and, of course, that of my Nana Harry – whose name was Gwen. God has truly blessed us all!)